...walk with me...

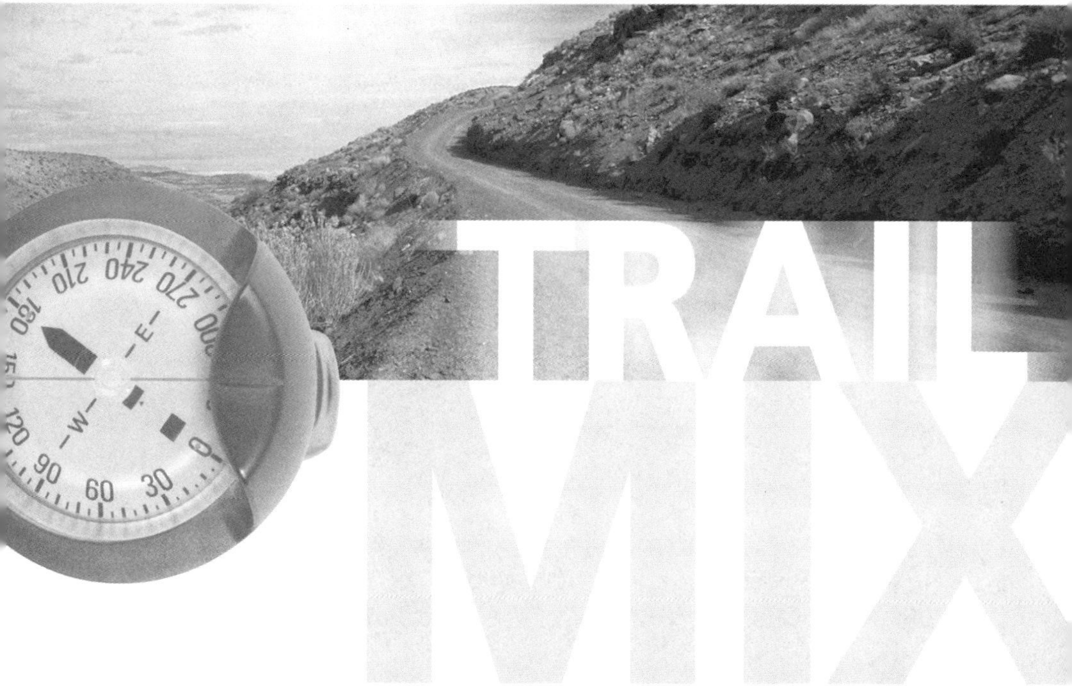

TRAIL MIX

Good Stuff for **Walk With Me** Teachers

Jessie Schut

Grand Rapids, Michigan

Any questions or comments about this book? We'd love to hear from you:

Faith Alive Christian Resources
1-800-333-8300
E-mail: editors@faithaliveresources.org

RCA Children's Ministry Office
1-800-968-3943
E-mail: childrensministry@rca.org

Presbyterians for Renewal
1-502-425-4630
E-mail: office@pfrenewal.org

Unless otherwise indicated, Scripture quotations are from the HOLY BIBLE: NEW INTERNATIONAL VERSION, © 1973, 1978, 1984 by International Bible Society. Used by permission of Zondervan Publishing House. All rights reserved.

Walk With Me curriculum has been developed by Faith Alive Resources in cooperation with the Children's Ministry Office of the Reformed Church in America and with Presbyterians for Renewal.

Trail Mix: Good Stuff for Walk With Me Teachers
Faith Alive Christian Resources published by CRC Publications.
© 2004 by CRC Publications, 2850 Kalamazoo Ave. SE, Grand Rapids, MI 49560. All rights reserved. Printed in the United States of America.

www.FaithAliveResources.org

ISBN 1-69255-193-9

10 9 8 7 6 5 4 3 2 1

Contents

Introduction 5

Hello
1   Top Ten Reasons to Walk With Me 8
2   Finding True North 10
3   What It Means to Walk With Me: A Kid's-Eye View 12
4   Do You Have What It Takes? 14
5   A Supply Checklist 16
6   The World Kids Come From 18
7   What Are They Doing Here? 20

Know
8   The Answer Is Always Jesus 22
9   Did Adam and Eve Have a Belly Button? And Other Questions
    Kids Ask 24
10 Many Trails, One Goal (Part 1) 26
11 Many Trails, One Goal (Part 2) 28
12 Mix It Up! 30
13 Discipline to Discipleship: A Matter of the Heart 32
14 Discipline to Discipleship: A Matter of Understanding 34
15 First Aid Kit 36
16 Who Wants a Pickle for a Teacher? 38
17 Charting the Course: Outlines and Lesson Plans 40
18 Just a Minute 42
19 Funky Funday School 44
20 Talk to Me! 46
21 Listen Up! 48

22	Move It!	50
23	Roll 'Em: Using Technology in the Classroom	52
24	Tales Around the Fire: The Art of Storytelling	54
25	No-No's: Abuse Prevention Guidelines	56
26	Walking Hand in Hand: Affirming Diversity	58
27	Signs of Life: Using Rituals and Symbols	60
28	Teaching Children to Pray	62

Grow

29	Taking Stock	64
30	Real Teachers Do Eat Crow: Dealing with Failures	66
31	Scout's Honor: The Need for Honesty and Transparency	68
32	Rest Stops: Remember to Take a Breather	70
33	Power Walking: Cultivating a Prayer Life	72
34	Stretching Keeps You Limber	74

Show

35	Pack Out What You Pack In	76
36	Learning the Ropes: Helping Kids Develop Their Spiritual Gifts	78
37	Unplug the Teaching Machine	80
38	Trail Blazing: A Look at the Future	82

Introduction

You've said yes to the awesome job of teaching children. This book, as its title suggests, is one of the tools you can use to help fulfill your commitment.

Trail Mix is a mixture of information and encouragement. As you sample it, you'll be reviewing the nuts and bolts of ministry with children and young teens. Some days, when the going seems easy, it can provide a nourishing and refreshing snack along the way; other days, when the trail seems steep and long, you'll want to grab some for a much-needed power boost.

After all, you've agreed to accompany children on their faith journey, and that journey has many twists and turns, ups and downs, and stops. Children grow and change in their spiritual needs, just as they do in their everyday life. Consider what it means to accompany children through the various stages of growth.

- "Walk with me!" says the uncertain preschooler as she approaches her first day in kindergarten. "Hold my hand so I won't be scared."
- "Walk with me!" says the excited little boy just learning to ride his bike. "I need to feel you nearby so I won't fall."
- "Walk with me!" says the happy second grader whose mom is accompanying a class field trip. "I'm so glad you're sharing this experience with me."
- "Walk with me!" says the confident fourth grader. "Watch what I can do and cheer me on."
- "Walk with me!" says the anxious adolescent. "I have so many questions, and I need someone to listen and help me sort out the truth."

Walk with me, say the children of the church. Show me Jesus. Answer my questions. Cheer me on. Share my joy. Wipe away my tears and help me to learn what being a Christian is all about. You've been invited to accompany kids on a journey of faith, to walk with them as they discover the truths of God's Word and make it their own.

May your walk with these children be a blessing to you and to them. May you experience traveling mercies with God as your guide. May you discover new sights and insights, and gain fresh energy from this journey. And may *Trail Mix* be a helpful source of strength along the way.

Dip into this book as you need it, or read through it in one sitting. Whatever works for you is fine. Like *Walk With Me* curriculum, it's divided into sections:

- **Hello:** an introduction to the art and craft of teaching, preparing you for the journey.
- **Know:** practical teaching tips and techniques to help your journey go more smoothly.
- **Grow:** thoughts and ideas that develop the bigger picture.
- **Show:** helping children become lifelong travelers on the faith journey.

Some who read this will be novices, for whom every word is a revelation; others will be veteran travelers who simply need a reminder of what to expect. Sometimes this book may be a salve for blistered feet, other times a signpost to new adventures. Occasionally, it may be a road map that shows where you've left the trail.

Our prayer is that it will bless your journey.

Top Ten Reasons to Walk With Me

1. **God said so.** "These commandments that I give you today are to be upon your hearts. Impress them on your children. Talk about them when you sit at home and when you walk along the road, when you lie down and when you get up" (Deut. 6:6-7). God's plan for passing on the good news of salvation has always been to tell the story person to person, from generation to generation. You're part of God's grand plan.

2. **It's what Jesus would do.** Jesus picked out a small ragtag group of followers and taught them the Way. And they went out and did the same . . . and so on, and so on. If each one reaches some and teaches some, the kingdom of God will spread on earth.

3. **The church needs you.** In fact, the church needs all its members to do what God has gifted them to do, from stoking the furnace to preaching the Word. If you have been gifted with a love of children and an ability to communicate with them, the church needs you to do your job of ministering to its youngest members.

4. **The kids need you.** Today's kids have such busy, stimulating lives that there's hardly any room for God. Can God compete with exciting stuff like computer games and videos, basketball and marching band? But you know a secret: our God is so big, so strong and so mighty, there's nothing our God cannot do. That's your story, and you're sticking to it. That's the story kids need to hear.

5. **You need this experience.** Oh yeah? you may ask. True, nobody said the job would be easy. Neither is a backpacking trip around Europe or a trek to the Himalayas. Anyone who's traveled, however, knows that such challenges broaden your horizons, strengthen your backbone, and create lifelong memories. The experience of teaching children will enrich you in ways you can't imagine right now.

6. **Society needs you.** "You are the salt of the world," said Jesus to his followers. And what the world desperately needs now is a liberal sprinkling of salt to preserve what's good and keep it from spoiling. God's message of love and forgiveness is that kind of salt. The more Christians spread that message, the stronger and healthier our society will be.

7. **You're part of a very big picture.** You're not just a drudge on the Sunday school assembly line. One person like you being used by God can change the world . . . just think of godly leaders like Tony Campolo and Dwight Moody. A good Sunday school teacher led each of them to the Lord, and they in turn taught thousands more. You may never know what a difference your words and love made, but God knows the big picture.

8. **To teach is to learn twice.** Wondering if you're really "spiritual" enough to teach others? God has a funny cure for that: if you want to grow spiritually, don't run away from teaching, commit yourself to it. As you prepare your lessons and then speak of what you learned, God will do a number on you. You're going to be blessed.

9. **Childhood is the teachable time.** Tobacco companies know if they can get kids hooked on cigarettes early, there's a huge chance they'll stay hooked. Statistics for the church are similar. A study by Barna Research Institute shows that most decisions to follow Christ are made before age twelve. After age eighteen, there is only a 4 percent chance that a person will become a committed Christian. Childhood is the teachable time, and you have the privilege of being there!

10. **You will make a whole lot of new friends.** The Sunday school superintendent will think you're the best thing going because you said yes. Parents will love you because you're showing an interest in their kids. The church will appreciate you because you are using your gifts. Kids you never knew before will grin and wave at you in church. And it can't get a lot better than that!

Finding True North

A compass is a handy thing when you're hiking in the wilderness, headed for a certain mountaintop that you know is somewhere north. Suddenly you realize you're lost. You take a bearing to find out where north is, and it shows which direction to go.

Sometimes when you're teaching a group of children you can feel exactly like a hiker: lost in the wilderness!

The first question you'll need to ask yourself is this: Where am I headed? You can't arrive at a destination if you don't know where you're going. Even a kindergarten kid knows that much. So where are you headed with your group of kids? Do you know your final destination?

Consider the effort you'll be putting into teaching the children this year. Which of these outcomes will be your aim?
- The children had a great time and remember church with fondness.
- You've made lots of new young friends.
- Your kids will always remember the Bible stories you told.
- Your group became a caring community.
- Boy, do those kids know their memory work!

Good stuff! Great outcomes!

But there's one more thing you need to know about a compass: there are two norths: a magnetic north, which wanders a bit according to the magnetic field, and a true north, which never changes. Heading for magnetic north may lead you off the trail and far away from your destination.

The true north of teaching Sunday school is not just fun, friendship, and Bible knowledge. True north is nurturing faith in children so that they grow to be full-fledged followers of Jesus.

Now there's a mountaintop to head for!

One final tip—and a word of encouragement—that most hikers know and have already experienced. You won't always hit exactly what you're looking for all the time. Expect to get a little lost occasionally.

But go for your destination. With God as your guide, you can trust that you're on the right track.

3 What It Means to Walk With Me: A Kid's-Eye View

Dear Teacher,

So, my folks tell me I'm going to Sunday school again this year. That's OK, that's cool. Let's have fun together this year.

Are you ready to walk with me on my faith journey? Here's what I hope will happen:

1. I hope you'll love me like nobody's business. You don't have to be the greatest singer or storyteller or craft expert, but you do have to love me lots. I hear that's what Jesus did, even when his disciples disappointed him.

2. I hope you'll show me that Jesus is living in your heart and that he's changed your life. And I hope you'll want to tell me about it. If it's real for you, I'm going to want to try it too. If it's not real for you, don't come . . . please!

3. I hope you know how to laugh. I've heard that laughter is the shortest distance between two people. What are you going to do if the bottle of glue tips over in your purse or the story poster falls down on the floor? When we laugh together, I feel good about life and good about being in Sunday school.

4. I hope you'll be able to go with the flow. Once my friend came to Sunday school so sad because his grandma had just died. We didn't have a lesson that day. Instead, we made paper flowers to put on her grave, and we talked about heaven. We all felt better afterward.

5. I hope you won't think my faith is not as good as your faith. I know I have lots to learn because I'm just starting out on this walk. But Jesus said grown-ups should have childlike trust too, and that must mean something. Can you show me that there's a kid inside you too?

6. I hope you'll expect the best from me. Sure, I might crab and whine when you raise the bar, but secretly I'll be pleased that you think I can grow to be the best I can possibly be.

7. I hope you'll understand where I'm coming from. Kids haven't got all the thinking and physical skills grown-ups have. Try to look at the world from my point of view before you figure out what I need to learn.

8. I hope we get to move around and do things instead of always listening and being quiet. Doing, moving, talking, looking . . . those are important ways of learning, and they come naturally to me.

There's more, but I'm sure you get the idea. And thanks for offering to walk with me . . . I hope you learn as much as I do on this journey.

Love,

Your kid

4 Do You Have What It Takes?

Quick. Think of a memorable teacher you've had, someone who's made a difference in your life. Why is this teacher one you'll never forget? Write down three characteristics:

1. _____

2. _____

3. _____

If you're like most people, you might have written down things like these:
- She really cared about me.
- He had a great sense of humor.
- Mr. Bell had a passion for the Bible—he made it come alive.
- She challenged me to be a better person.

Notice what's not on the list?
- He could recite Psalm 119 from beginning to end.
- She kept good attendance records.
- His classroom was always neat and tidy.

That's because it's the character of the teacher you usually remember rather than specific skills. And that's the way it should be, for character begins in the heart and spirit in lives transformed by God's grace—which is what your teaching is all about.

A wise person once said you only need three loves and two skills to be a good teacher.

What are the three loves?
- Love God.
- Love the ones you teach.
- Love what you teach: God's Word.

What are the two skills?
- Be able to communicate effectively.
- Be able to create a community in your classroom.

As you read this book, you'll notice that many readings include specific ideas on how to grow the two skills. Note especially the Know and Show sections.

However, nobody can teach you the three loves. If you have what it takes, you and the Holy Spirit will never stop working together to grow in grace and love.

Then someday, somewhere, some grown-up children of God will remember and tell others about a memorable teacher they once had. That could be you!

5 A Supply Checklist

Before hikers hit the trail, they double-check their supply list. They don't want to be stuck some moonless night on a trail without a flashlight. That could be disastrous, especially in a skunk-infested forest.

In the same way, before you begin walking the faith journey with children, you'd better become familiar with your travel gear and be sure you know how to use it. After all, there are some little stinkers out there!

Here's what you need to pack:

1. Bible

This is the most important part of your gear, your compass. Without it you'd be lost. You are teaching God's holy Word, not merely Sunday school stories from a manual. As you prepare your lessons each week, read the story *first* from Scripture and meditate on it. Plant God's Word in your heart like a seed; be assured it will grow and bear fruit.

2. Leader's Guide

Don't leave home without it! A leader's guide is like having someone plan your itinerary, and that's a helpful thing in unfamiliar territory. In the classroom, it's like having an experienced teacher standing beside you, whispering in your ear. Together you'll make a fine team. After you've meditated on Scripture and prayed for insight, read through the lesson background (Word-Search) in your guide to help you understand the passage. Check out the recommended steps and options, and choose those that you believe will best meet your group's needs and personality. By all means substitute your own ideas if they're better: a leader's guide is *not* infallible or exclusive.

3. Leader's Resources

Travelers stuff their packs with necessities like money, a water bottle, aspirin and bandages, and extra rolls of TP to make the trip easier. In the same way, your gear will include leader's resources—pictures, posters, patterns, templates, CDs, and so on—that make your job easier and add interest and variety. Get familiar with your leader's resources and use these aids shamelessly.

*4. Volunteers

An old American spiritual says, "You gotta walk that lonesome valley, you gotta walk it by yourself," but that's not what children's church school is all about. You are part of a faith community that includes many different gifts and abilities. If retiree Mr. Sam is a great storyteller, invite him to impersonate Moses for a few sessions—kids will never forget his memorable first-person stories. If Nate is a teen with energy to burn, invite him to burn it by helping with crafts or videotaping one of your sessions.

5. Knee Pads

You're going to be spending a lot of time on your knees in prayer. In all of your work, depend on God; look to God for strength and wisdom. God will never let you down. (See pp. 62-63 and 72-73 for more about prayer.)

*Two important rules for using volunteers: 1. Ask well in advance of the need to give a volunteer a chance to prepare. 2. Always have children thank people who share their gifts with your group.

6   The World Kids Come From

You may be wondering, "Just who are these kids I'll be teaching?"

If you were to create a composite snapshot of a "typical" kid in your group, you'd have to start with this reality: he or she lives in a postmodern world where truth is relative, authority is questioned, change is exponential, and life is assumed to be messy and unpredictable. Postmodern thinking offers no neat and tidy boxes to hold community, family, truth, morals, values, communication modes, and institutions. Life is unpredictable, and today's stability is tomorrow's outdated reality.

Add these sobering statistics into the mix:

- One out of every six households in North America moves every year.
- Two out of three preschoolers live in homes where the TV is usually left on at least half the time, even if no one is watching; one-third live in homes where the TV is on "almost all" or "most" of the time (from a study done by the Henry J. Kaiser Family Foundation).
- Nearly 20 percent of 12-14 year olds report having had sex (www.teenpregnancy.org).
- Computers, the Internet, chat rooms, e-mail, Instant Messaging, cell phones, and text messaging are staples for many children and teens.
- Approximately 39 percent of the homeless are children (Urban Institute, 2000).
- The proportion of children ages 6 to 18 that were overweight increased from 6 percent in 1976-1980 to 15 percent in 1999-2000. The report suggested that eating out, diets low in fruits and vegetables, and lack of exercise probably play a role (National Institute of Child Health and Human Development, News Release July 18, 2003).

- Half of all children (in the U.S.) will witness the breakup of a parent's marriage. Of these, close to half will also see the breakup of a parent's second marriage. Forty percent of children growing up in America today are being raised without their fathers. Statistics for Christians and non-Christians are pretty much the same (www.nappaland.org).
- A Blue Cross/Blue Shield 2001 survey of 10- to 17-year-olds showed that half the children interviewed were "aware" of sports supplements and drugs, and one in five takes them, less for athletic enhancement than to look more attractive to the opposite sex.
- The National Youth Suicide Prevention Center in Washington, D.C., reports that every hour of every day 228 teenagers in the United States will attempt to take their own lives. Between 6,000 and 20,000 teens will succeed.

A Christian website describes Millennials (kids/young people born in the 1980s and 1990s) this way: "Their multi-media driven world tries to influence them in every way. They've learned to be skeptical, they don't take anything for granted. They're also spiritually hungry. They are from a world of broken marriages, broken homes, and broken dreams. They've witnessed broken churches" (www.youth-impact.org).

In other words, there is no typical kid in your class. Sally comes from a middle-class home where she lives with her mom and younger brother; Juan's family will only be in the neighborhood for a year while his dad is on sabbatical; Melissa's sister is under doctor's care as she battles with anorexia; Michael and his dad are living with his grandparents until his dad finds a job; and Andrew's pager interrupts your lesson several times until you ask him to turn it off.

But all these kids have something in common: Jesus loves them very much and wants to make his home in their hearts. And that's the most important thing you need to know!

7   What Are They Doing Here?

Why do kids come to Sunday school? With Internet, TV, sports, school activities, friends, music lessons, and family, kids' lives today are pretty crowded. So why do they still come?

And then there's a second question: Is it time well spent? Is it worth the time and effort and money we put into it? Can't parents teach their children about God?

A survey done by the Barna Research Group (May 2003) revealed that 85 percent of parents of children under age 13 believe they have the primary responsibility for teaching their children about religious beliefs and spiritual matters, and 96 percent believe it's their job to teach their children values.

Here's the kicker, though: "Related research revealed that a majority of parents do not spend *any* time during a typical week discussing religious matters or studying religious materials with their children" (Barna Research Online).

Clearly, the church has a role to play in the spiritual development of children. Many parents do take their children to church and are willing to let the church provide them with religious instruction.

So who's teaching the children about God? Could it be TV? The average American youth spends about 1,023 hours watching television (that's 100+ hours more than they spend in school!) In one year, that child will see 20,000 commercials, many of them for junk food and toys. But he probably won't learn much about a God who loves him enough to sacrifice his Son.

Ditto for the Internet, chat rooms, video games, and sports activities.

Do you still wonder if you are important? Do you wonder if you have a job to do? Don't doubt for a moment that you've been chosen to do a very special job: to declare God's love and to invite children to come home to their heavenly Father.

*I'm chewing on the morsel of a proverb;
I'll let you in on the sweet old truths,
stories we heard from our fathers,
counsel we learned at our mother's knee.
We're not keeping this to ourselves,
we're passing it along to the next generation—
God's fame and fortune,
the marvelous things he has done.
He planted a witness in Jacob,
set his Word firmly in Israel,
then commanded our parents
to teach it to their children
so the next generation would know,
and all the generations to come—
know the truth and tell the stories
so their children can trust in God,
never forget the works of God
but keep his commands to the letter.*
—Psalm 78:2-7, *The Message*

8. The Answer Is Always Jesus

You know the scene: at the end of the Bible story, you ask a question.

Before the words are actually out of your mouth, several children are already wildly waving their arms in the air. They may not hear the question, but they know the answer: Jesus. In church, the answer to any question is always Jesus. Or God.

Who healed the blind man?
Jesus.
Who listens to our prayers?
Jesus.
Who wore a coat of many colors?
Jesus. Oops . . . hmm. I guess that was Joseph.

If you're getting a lot of "Jesus" responses or pat answers in your class, a quick primer on questioning techniques may help:

1. Remember and use these three kinds of questions:
- Questions for information review the content of the story or session and are generally factual. Who healed the blind man? How many people did Jesus feed? Name three disciples.
- Questions for explanation dig deeper into the content, inviting kids to draw inferences and process ideas. What was unusual about Abraham's journey? How did Peter's life change after he became Jesus' follower?
- Questions for application ask children to ponder the importance of this story or session in their own lives. If you were in the boat with Jesus and the fishermen, would you have been frightened of the storm? What kinds of situations are frightening to you right now? Can you trust Jesus to still the storm?

Always plan your questions before teaching, and make sure to address each of the different levels of understanding.

2. Ask open-ended questions that may not have any right answers, and that may lead to more questions. For instance, "wondering" questions like these invite open-ended reflection and thoughtfulness rather than neat and tidy responses: I wonder whether anyone can do the things that Jesus did . . . or, I wonder how Jeremiah felt when he was thrown into a deep, dark pit. . . .

3. Your body language can encourage children to think more deeply.
- Keep your eyes moving around the room as you ask the question. If you focus just on one person, the other children will tune out.
- After you've asked the question, lower your eyes to the floor or table for 15 seconds or more and be silent. By not making eye contact, you are giving thoughtful children the opportunity to think through the answer, and giving the "Jesus is the answer" kids time to reconsider.

4. Accept each answer as the gift it is. When children offer answers to your questions, they make themselves vulnerable to teasing or laughing if the answer is wrong. So even if the answer is way off base, affirm the child's courage. Say something like, "Good try" or "Thanks for thinking about that." If necessary, deflect the spotlight to yourself by saying, "Maybe my question is hard to understand. Let me rephrase it."

5. Never ask a question you are not willing to try to answer yourself. You're a fellow traveler, not a tester or census taker.

6. If you don't have an answer to a question, don't be afraid to say so. By saying, "I don't know, but I'm going to try and find out," you're modeling the concept that the Christian journey is one of constant learning and growing.

So, who loves teachers and kids very much? Who is pleased to see God's kids struggling together to ask big questions? Who said, "Ask, and it will be given to you; seek, and you will find; knock, and the door will be opened to you"?

You know the answer, don't you? The answer is Jesus.

9 Did Adam and Eve Have a Belly Button? And Other Questions Kids Ask

This may be a tough pill to swallow, but you need to hear the truth: You may not get to ask all the questions you've so carefully planned as part of your lesson.

That's the bad news. But here's the good news: Don't worry . . . kids will ask lots of questions of their own.

Did Adam and Eve have a belly button? Who did Cain marry? How big was Goliath? What's heaven like? What does adultery mean? Is it true that if you see God, you'll die?

That's for starters. If kids trust you enough, they'll begin asking the "big gun" questions: If Jesus doesn't like divorce, why did my dad, who is a Christian, leave my mom? Does it hurt to die? If God loves everybody, why did he let the terrorists fly airplanes into the World Trade Center towers? Do Hindu babies go to heaven?

They'll ask you these questions because being a kid isn't all fun and games. It's about growing and learning; it's about being bombarded by information that's tough to sort out and understand. It's about living in the real world, where bad things happen as well as good. It's about needing a place where someone will listen and enter their world and give them the answers to the questions that keep them up at night.

Hopefully, they're asking their parents these questions, too. But consider the statistics: a study conducted by the American Family Research Council in 1990 revealed that the average time *per week* that parents spend in meaningful conversation with their children is just over 38 minutes. Your group, meeting weekly, can be a wonderful support to busy and harried parents.

Sunday school classes are uniquely suited as places to ask good questions.

Consider these factors:

- Your class gathers together children of similar ages who are dealing with similar developmental issues (unlike families, where children are spread across a wider age range).
- Your chief purpose is to focus on faith issues, the nuts and bolts of life.
- Classes are often small enough to become a safe community where children can explore spiritual issues.
- Sunday school teachers are fellow faith travelers who love children and are committed to helping them grow and learn.

Will you know all the answers to kids' questions? No. Do you need to have all the answers? No! But by listening carefully, asking your own questions to help children clarify their ideas, and giving opportunities for children to explore issues together, you're teaching them huge concepts.

In effect, you're showing children that the faith journey is a dynamic, growing, ever-changing road trip, that God invites us to wrestle with him, and that church is a place where you can take your questions and doubts safely, knowing your faith family will support you.

Along the way, they may even discover that Adam and Eve did indeed have belly buttons . . . didn't they?

Many Trails, One Goal (Part 1)

God didn't use a cookie cutter to make people all the same size and shape, with all the same aptitudes, abilities, and ideas.

Instead, we are created in God's own image. Like a prism, all of us reflect little bits and pieces of the wonderful and infinite possibilities within God. What a gift and a blessing!

But from a teacher's point of view, what a puzzle! Little Trevor fidgets and twists during storytelling time, but he loves to act out a drama. Jeannie, on the other hand, listens with rapt attention to your story, but shrinks if she's asked to perform.

Jason really digs puzzles in the take-home paper, but he tunes out whenever your group sings. Su-Lin loves to draw and paint, but she gets disruptive during a quiet prayer activity. Every one of your kids seems to have a different "favorite" activity. What's that all about?

What it's all about is "multiple intelligences." Not only do children—and adults—have different personalities and their own preferred learning styles, but they also have leading intelligences that they prefer to use to solve problems and learn new material.

Traditionally, a child's intelligence was measured chiefly on linguistic and mathematical abilities. But multiple intelligence theory says there are many ways to be intelligent. A star hockey player may not be gifted verbally, but he's always in the right place to grab the puck and put it in the net. He is body smart. A budding artist may have real difficulty figuring out math problems, but her anti-smoking poster wins a national award. She's picture smart.

Here's a list of the eight intelligences observed by researchers—see if you can associate each with a child or children in your group:

- **Word Smart** (linguistic intelligence): sensitive to the sounds, meaning, and functions of words and language; loves storytelling, writing, reading, chanting, poetry.
- **Math Smart** (logical-mathematical intelligence): is able to discern logical or numerical patterns and can reason through puzzles and problems; loves counting, classifying, puzzle-solving.
- **Picture Smart** (spatial intelligence): is able to use visual impressions in creative ways, can perceive and learn best through pictures and symbols; loves art work, design, inventing, creating.
- **Body Smart** (bodily-kinesthetic intelligence): good at controlling body movements and handling objects skillfully; loves to do crafts, participate in athletics, do drama, dance and sculpture.
- **Music Smart** (musical intelligence): is able to produce and appreciate rhythm and pitch, appreciates the forms of musical expression; loves singing, playing instruments, rhythmic activities, listening to music.
- **People Smart** (interpersonal intelligence): is able to feel and respond to moods and motivations of others, sensitive to others' feelings; loves to lead, help, create community, work in groups.
- **Self Smart** (intrapersonal intelligence): sensitive to one's own feelings and emotions, self-aware of strengths and weaknesses; loves to participate in rituals, sharing groups, discuss religious ideas and psychological theories.
- **Earth Smart** (naturalist intelligence): sensitivity to creation and what it teaches, aware of the interrelatedness of life, observant of natural rhythms; loves to examine nature, be outdoors, observe growth and change, link natural phenomena.

Although people generally have one or two leading intelligences—that is, the way they learn best—each person in your group possesses some degree of all eight intelligences. So there's no need to create eight different lesson plans to reach all the kids in your class!

But since God made us like this—infinite in variety and learning capacities—doesn't it make sense to help children grow in faith by using a variety of learning experiences? In doing so, we are honoring the image of God in each child.

Note: For more information and practical applications of multiple intelligences theory, check out page 28.

Many Trails, One Goal (Part 2)

"Reach everyone you teach" ought to be a guiding principle for Sunday school teachers. It means that in every session you'll try to offer learning activities that appeal to all the different learning styles (intelligences) we've been talking about.

Sound like a tough job? Not really. A good curriculum will incorporate multiple intelligence theory into its structure and provide you with a variety of approaches and learning opportunities. *Walk With Me* labels each of its steps to show which intelligences are used in the suggested teaching strategies.

The biggest obstacle to teaching to the multiple intelligences is the mistaken notion that words are the main channel through which children learn. Teachers often believe it is their job to talk and the children's job to listen. Research shows that in traditional classrooms, teachers talk their way through 70 percent of class time.

So if you've ever had a good teaching idea and then wondered if it was just too much fun to be a good learning strategy, think again! Consider all of these ways of learning that will, in some way, reach every one you teach. Notice that many of the activities reach several intelligences at once.

Word Smart — brainstorming, choral reading, word games, storytelling, writing journal responses, tape recording children's ideas, publishing a newspaper.

Example: Children tape record their prayers for a sick member of the congregation and send it to her with cards of encouragement. (Also People Smart, Self Smart, Picture Smart)

Number Smart — classifying, sorting into lists, graphing, counting, creating and using codes, logic puzzles and games, arranging facts in sequence.

Example: Children poll each other to discover who is their favorite Bible hero. (Also People Smart, Self Smart)

 Picture Smart — doing photography, creating models and dioramas, working with Play-Doh and other art materials, using symbols, finding patterns, visualization exercises.

Example: Children build the walls of Jericho with shoeboxes. (Also People Smart, Number Smart)

 Body Smart — creative movement, dramatization, pantomime, playing active games, doing crafts, cooking, using sign language, hands-on activities, stretching and relaxing.

Example: Children do a trust walk with a partner while blindfolded. (Also Self Smart, People Smart)

 Music Smart — singing, humming, whistling, listening to music, using rhythm instruments, chanting and rapping, learning memory work in song.

Example: Children clap a rhythm while learning memory verse. (Also Body Smart, Word Smart)

 People Smart — participating in cooperative group activities, peer teaching, playing board games, forming clubs, having parties and celebrations, acting out roles, people sculpting.

Example: Children work in small groups to develop a list of five questions for reviewing the story. (Also Word Smart, Number Smart)

 Self Smart — doing independent study, taking one-minute reflection periods, contemplative praying, choosing activities or interest centers, writing journal responses, working in private spaces.

Example: Children are given a choice of writing in their journals or creating a piece of art as a response to the storytelling. (Also Word Smart, Picture Smart)

 Earth Smart — taking nature walks, having plants and pets in the classroom, using discovery tables, doing experiments, using nature posters for decor, recording observations from classroom windows, weather watching.

Example: Children check out whether objects will sink or float in a tub of water before listening to the story of Peter's attempt to walk on water. (Also Body Smart, People Smart, Number Smart)

12 Mix It Up!

You've heard the saying "A change is as good as a rest." Is it true? Is change for change's sake beneficial?

Research suggests that it's true. There's a part of our brain (called Magoun's Brain) which seems to be stimulated by novelty. Christian educator Marlene LeFever tells of an industrial study on ways to increase production: "They added music and production went up. They added extra lighting and production went up. They took away music and production went up. They lowered the lighting and production went up. It became apparent that it wasn't the individual changes that made the difference. It was change itself" (*Creative Teaching Methods,* Cook Communications, 1985, 1996).

This is good news for teachers. It doesn't seem to matter what the change—any change will make a difference. When you mix it up, kids will sit up and take notice. They'll become more engaged in learning.

Here's an alphabet of learning strategies that will stimulate your kids—pick one you've not tried in your class before and check it out for yourself:

A. acrostics, art work, aquariums, assignments, animal care

B. book nook, board games, banners, brainstorming, bulletin boards, blindfold activities

C. choral readings, classifying, cooking, cross-age tutoring, case studies, charts, contests, computer games, crafts, cameras, codes

D. drama, dioramas, debates, data collection, drawing, drumming, decor change, desk rearrangement, dance, demonstrations, discussions

E. evaluations, exhibits, eco-studies, earth watch activities, early-bird prizes

F. field trips, films, flash cards, feel-and-guess, fish bowl, faith walk

G. games, graphic symbols, graphs, gardening, group singing, group projects, goal setting, guests

H. hymn-sing, hands-on activities, heart commitments

I. individual projects, illustrations, interest centers, interviews, independent study

J. journals, joke books, junk sculptures, judging, journey of faith map

K. kinesthetic activities such as tracing, body movements, sign language, tiptoeing, prayer walk

L. letter writing, logic puzzles, listening to music, listening games, Lego constructions, laughter

M. mime, manipulatives, mood music, microscope, maps, memory work, mobiles, murals, models, magic tricks

N. nature walk, neighborhood survey, newspaper clipping, number games

O. optical illusions, options, overheads, object lessons, oral reports, one-minute challenge, open house

P. painting, panel discussion, pantomime, photography, peer sharing, peer support groups, people sculpting, pets in the classroom, plants, puppets, puzzles, parties

Q. quizzes, question of the week, question box, quilting, quiet time

R. rhythm instruments, rhyming, rest periods, research, rebus, role plays, review games, relaxation activities, raps

S. storytelling, sand table, sports, Scripture search, service projects, skits, stained-glass windows, surveys, science experiments, simulations, sign language

T. tape recording, typewriters, testimonies, tactile materials, task forces

U. updating current events board, unison singing, underlining, unit project, uniform design for the class, U-pick activity time, use examples

V. video, visualization, visual aids, voting, Venn diagrams, venting bulletin board, values exercise, vigil of prayer

W. workshop, worksheets, word games, word association, weather observations

X. eXercise, eXclamations, eXcitement

Y. yard clean-up, yeast experiment, yodeling, yarn creations, yearbook, youth manifesto

Z. zany Bible costume contest, zither demonstration (OK, we're scraping the bottom of the barrel here!)

There you have it: almost 200 ways to add zing to your session. Mix it up!

13 Discipline to Discipleship: A Matter of the Heart

Discipline /'disiplin/*noun:* 1. A system of rules used to maintain control over people 2. Punishment, reprimand.

If your idea of discipline matches this dictionary definition, think again. In the dictionary and also in a Sunday school classroom, the word *disciple* comes before *discipline.* The root word for both words is the Latin *discere,* meaning to learn.

Learning, not punishment, is what discipline is all about.

- Your ultimate purpose for discipline is training and teaching, not justice or revenge.
- Your focus is the future (teaching alternative behavior), not the past (punishing poor behavior).
- Your attitude is disappointment and love, not anger and frustration.

Classroom discipline is important not merely to maintain control and order in the classroom, but also to help kids to become more and more Christ-like in thought, word, and deed.

Perhaps a better definition of discipline, especially in the Sunday school classroom, is this: "Training of the heart and mind that produces growth that reflects the image of God."

Discipline is not an option. By recognizing its importance in your teaching, you demonstrate that you love your kids enough to care about their future. It's what God does with us. Consider Paul's words: "My son, do not make light of the Lord's discipline, and do not lose heart when he rebukes you, because the Lord disciplines those he loves, and he punishes everyone he accepts as a son. . . . Our fathers disciplined us for a little while as they thought best, but God disciplines us for our good, that we may share in his holiness" (Heb. 12:5b, 6, 10).

The core of good classroom discipline lies in the heart—that is, *your* heart.

You may have heard that teachers need to carry a big stick (figuratively, of course). But that's not nearly as effective as having a big heart. Do you like children? Do you respect their strengths and try to build them up where they are weak? Do you dream of them becoming all that they can be? Do you want to show them Jesus' love? Are you a model of what you hope they will learn, reading the Bible and praying for the children daily? Then you have the foundation for good classroom discipline and for creating an environment where children can learn.

Discipline to Discipleship: A Matter of Understanding

If the core of good classroom discipline lies in the heart, the layers surrounding the core come out of understanding and knowledge. And you'll need both heart and knowledge to maintain effective discipline in your group.

You might love your kids like nobody's business, but they can still run all over you. And you might get all kinds of warm fuzzies thinking about them, but you'll also need to know how to handle them. You'll need to understand what techniques will help you maintain order and a stress-free environment.

First, you should understand the importance of preparation. Your motto should be "Prepare and Prevent" rather than "Repair and Repent." Prepared teachers feel more comfortable in their role. They are able to give kids more attention because they aren't spending precious minutes putting last-minute details together. Prepared teachers know what they want to accomplish; their goals provide direction and momentum in the classroom. Prepared teachers think about their kids as they plan their lessons, anticipating possible problems and making contingency plans. Prepared teachers think about each child's needs and shape the session to meet those needs.

Spending time in preparation means you are disciplining yourself. You're becoming a model of what you expect of your children.

The second aspect of understanding involves knowing basic techniques for maintaining order in the classroom. Workshops and teacher training seminars can give you many helpful pointers, so take advantage of them if you have the opportunity. Share stories with other teachers to find out what they find effective. Consider the following:

1. **Gear teaching to children's attention spans,** about one minute for each year. Expecting a five-year old to listen to a ten-minute story without involving him in movement or response is asking for trouble.

2. **Gear teaching to a child's level.** Bored or frustrated children will look for something else to do, and usually that's not a good thing! Know the characteristics of your age group, and make sure your activities, vocabulary, and expectations are appropriate.

3. **State a few basic expectations clearly, then enforce them consistently.** You cannot assume children know what you expect, so state the things that are important to you at the outset. But keep rules to the minimum, or you'll be spending all your time being a traffic cop instead of a teacher. Involve your children in establishing and enforcing basic rules.

4. **Engrave this watchword on your palms, where you'll see it often: variety.** Read pages 26-31 to understand the importance of incorporating a variety of activities into your sessions.

5. **Respect children's individuality and their need for dignity.** Yelling, physical restraint, and singling out offenders can cause alarm, shame, and feelings of violation. If a child is disruptive, speak to him or her in private to get at the root of the problem. Keep your voice down—the louder your speak, the louder kids' voices become.

6. **Expect the best!** Rejoice over good behavior. Catch 'em being good and reinforce that behavior.

You'll find that's a whole lot better than carrying a big stick!

Note: The quiz on pages 64 and 65 will help pinpoint areas of strength and weakness.

15 First Aid Kit

It's hard to listen to stories about Jesus, the bread of life, if there's a hunger in your belly for a piece of toast.

And stories about how Jesus protects us from danger won't make a big impact if you're scared of bullies in the church hallways.

Children need Jesus . . . but it's hard for them to meet him if their other needs aren't taken care of first. Eminent psychologist Abraham Maslow described the situation in his hierarchy of needs (see chart on p. 37). Some needs, he said, take precedence over others. Basic needs—the need for food, air, and water (physiological needs) and the need for security and freedom from fear (safety needs)—must be satisfied before a person can begin a quest to meet higher needs such as love, self-esteem, and achievement.

What does that mean for you as you teach? It means that you will be sensitive to your children's physical needs and ensure that their need for safety and security is satisfied.

Physical Needs

Hungry children are listless learners and lack ability to concentrate. If you're aware that some children in your group come to class hungry, consider these possibilities.

- If you suspect that some kids' families have financial difficulties, get your deacons involved. This isn't just your problem; it's a situation that belongs to the whole church.
- If kids are coming to class without breakfast because their families are too rushed Sunday mornings, you'll need to do some creative thinking. Can you tactfully alert parents to your problem and ask them to remedy the situation? Perhaps you can invite children to think of ways to solve this problem themselves.

- Young children and those going through growth spurts digest food quickly and are subject to rapid fluctuations in appetite. Consider serving a nutritious snack as part of every session. Be aware of any food allergies kids may have.

Safety Needs

These needs include security and stability; protection from harm; freedom from fear, anxiety, and chaos; structure, order, law, and limits. They can be met in the following ways:

- Make sure your church has (and enforces) a child safety policy. Such a policy stipulates procedures for screening teachers and helpers, for accompanying children to the bathroom, for physical standards for furniture and toys, and other protections for children. (For more information, see *Preventing Child Abuse,* Faith Alive Christian Resources.)
- If you become aware that a child in your group is being abused, you must report that abuse to your supervisors, and if need be, to community authorities.
- Gear classroom rules toward kids' physical and emotional safety, and enforce them consistently.
- Anticipate possible problems in order to prevent them from happening. Setting limits and giving specific instructions will prevent many accidents.
- Provide an environment that's free of anxiety and fear. Your attitude of acceptance and care and your zero-tolerance policy on peer ridicule and harrassment will make your classroom a safe community.

Jesus knew the importance of meeting physical needs and needs for safety and security. He fed the crowds when they were hungry and calmed the stormy seas. He reprimanded the Pharisees when they became abusive, and he protected the woman caught in an act of adultery. Most important, he offered his love, his forgiveness, and his Spirit to work in us so we can become all that he means us to be.

We are called to do likewise with the children in our care.

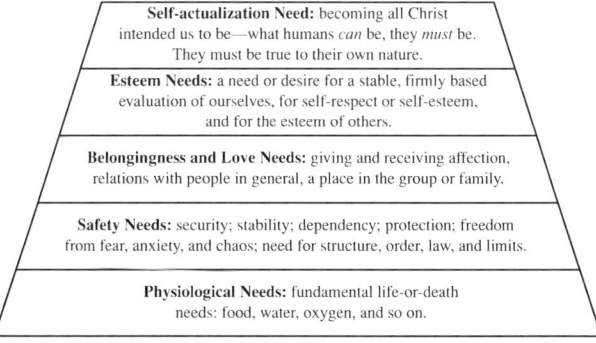

16 KNOW

Who Wants a Pickle for a Teacher?

If you want to build a healthy, happy atmosphere in your classroom, think *fun!*

Contrary to conventional thinking, fun is not the opposite of hard work or discipline. It is actually an essential ingredient to good teaching. Mary Poppins knew that when she sang, "Just a spoonful of sugar makes the medicine go down." Fun is like the yeast in a loaf of bread, the baking powder in a birthday cake, the helium in a hot-air balloon. Without it, you end up flat.

How do you add fun to your classroom?

1. Laugh! Did you know that laughter is the shortest distance between two people? As Brennan Manning says, "If the joy of the Lord is in your heart, please notify your face!" Show your children that life is a wonderful journey, not something to be endured till we get to heaven.

And let's face it . . . things will happen in your sessions that will make you want to cry . . . or laugh. What else are you going to do when the object lesson bombs or when the goat you brought in for the Christmas pageant does what goats do on the stage? Lighten up and enjoy: think of the stories you'll have to tell one day when you get past these experiences.

2. Play! Kids learn just about everything through play. They learn about shapes through puzzles and matching games; they learn about cooperation through playing with friends; they learn science by playing with water in the bathtub.

You can play with your group too: board games, contests, dramatization, raps, creative movement, search-and-find activities, guessing games, and more. *Walk With Me* has "fun" as one of its stated values and includes fun activities in every session.

3. Kids need change and stimulation . . . and they need routine and stability. That's a fine line to tread. But both can be fun if you keep 'em guessing. Add something unexpected or unusual to your classroom routine to make kids sit up and take notice. Imagine their reactions when they arrive in class to find several moms with little babies already there. They'll never forget that Jesus loves little children when these moms and tots act out the story. And they'll love holding and cuddling the little ones too. You can keep 'em guessing in many different ways: bringing in new items every week for a discovery table, inviting kids to lead part of the lesson, having guests give their testimonies, using ice-breaker activities . . . use your imagination!

4. Introduce fun routines that kids count on. Something as simple as a secret class handshake, a riddle of the week, or a weekly cartoon on the bulletin board—something kids know will happen, that they look forward to. One teacher always brings mints to pass out during the story time, another hands out a tacky pin to a kid of the week at the end of every session—the pin gets passed around to a different child each week.

5. Take kids out of the classroom. While the logistics may appear daunting, occasionally teach a lesson in a place other than a classroom. Imagine telling the story of Jesus feeding the five thousand in a community soup kitchen—afterward, kids chop up vegies for the soup. Tell the Christmas story in a barn. Hike with the children through a park as you act out the story of the Exodus. While you won't do this every week, such a change of scenery can reap wonderful rewards. And it's fun!

Who was the first tennis player in the Bible? Joseph: he served in Pharaoh's court.

What did Noah say when he finished loading the ark? "Now I've herded everything!"

Who was the most sorry when the prodigal son returned home? The fatted calf.

Charting the Course: Outlines and Lesson Plans

John's a passionate hiker. In his pack, he carries a notebook listing all the trails he hopes to hike before he dies. After each trip, he jots down notes about the trail he's conquered. He also carries a trail map and guidebook in his pack. They're indispensable tools in his quests. He knows that a successful hike depends as much on preparation and planning as on endurance, the right supplies, and a passion for walking.

Teachers can learn a lot from John. You may have the desire to teach (passion), a good curriculum (supplies), and health and strength to tackle the job (endurance), but you also need to plan and prepare. Aims and outlines will help you achieve success.

Aims

Hikers know their final destination before they begin a serious hike, and you should know what you're aiming for before you begin planning your lesson. If you aim at nothing, you're sure to hit it!

> **aim \ *noun* \ a clearly directed intent or purpose**

A good curriculum will state an aim for each step of the session. It may use words like goal or purpose rather than aim, but the intent is the same: to tell you what you hope to achieve in your teaching. For instance, the four steps in *Walk With Me* (Hello, Know, Grow, Show) are each prefaced by a stated goal ("The children will feel sure that Jesus loves them" or "The children will think of a way to show Jesus' love to a neighbor.")

Keep your aim in the back of your mind as you teach, always directing activities and discussions to help you achieve your aim.

Outlines

A lesson outline is like a road map: it keeps you from getting lost and charts your course so that you'll arrive at your destination.

You may think that your curriculum *is* your lesson outline, and you would be correct. Good curriculum is a wonderful tool—it provides thoughtful strategies devised by experienced teachers that will help you achieve the stated aims.

Walk With Me follows these steps:

- **Hello.** An attention-grabber; its purpose is preparing children for the Bible story.
- **Know.** Listening to God's Word: the center of your session.
- **Grow.** Reflecting on God's Word: kids consider what God is telling them in his Word.
- **Show.** Acting on God's Word: the lesson application, inviting kids to grow and change and put God's Word into practice.

But good curriculum is *only* a tool. After you've studied the Scripture passage and thought through what it means for you and for your children, you may realize that you have better ideas than the curriculum provides. Wonderful! Follow your heart and try them out on your kids! You know your children better than a curriculum writer does. You may be teaching a session about the healing of Jairus's daughter to a group of children who have lost a classmate in a car accident. They have needs and questions that may not be covered in your curriculum's strategies.

By using aims and outlines, you'll be following in the footsteps of an eminent teacher, the apostle Paul. He tells Timothy, "Stay right there on top of things so that the teaching stays on track.... The whole point of what we're urging is simply *love*" (1 Tim. 1:3a, 5a, *The Message*)

Those who fail to plan are planning to fail.

18. Just a Minute...

Think of all the earth-changing events that happen in less than a minute:
- Albert Einstein is born.
- Adolph Hitler is born
- The *Titanic* hits an iceberg.
- A shepherd boy throws a stone and discovers the Dead Sea Scrolls.
- The atom bomb is dropped on Nagasaki.
- A peace accord is signed.

Events and decisions that happen in less than a minute can change the world and affect peoples' lives forever.

The same is true in a classroom. What you do with just one minute can have a major impact on the rest of your session and on the kids in your group. Keep these principles in mind:

1. **You only have a minute to make a good first impression.**
Kids today live in a world of 60-second sound bites and news clips. If they don't like what they see in the first minute, they'll change the channel, stop the video, replace the computer game. In your classroom, they'll tune out.

So make the first minute of your classroom time count. What do kids see as they enter your room? A pleasant place that welcomes them or a boring, barren room? What do they hear as they enter? Sounds of welcome and joy or strident expressions of anxiety? What do you have planned to direct their thinking and engagement?

2. **Treat the teachable moment like pure gold.** Like Haley's Comet, it may not come around again for a long time.

When a teachable moment comes along, drop everything to tend to it. When Johnny asks why his grandpa died, when Susie asks for prayers for her sick sister, when Aya expresses distress about a situation he saw on the news, when Carlito carelessly utters a racial slur . . . that's when your teaching can take off. There's an immediacy and urgency in these situations that infuses your teaching with meaning. Children sit up and take notice because the teaching is attached to a real event in their lives. Jesus used every opportunity to speak at the teachable moments: you should, too.

3. Transitions can make or break a session.

You can lose a lot of kids between the Bible story and the response activity. Every time you move from one activity to the next, that golden first minute rears its head again.

So think about and plan how you will move from step to step in your session. Good curriculum will often include transitional statements or activities, signaling children that one part of the lesson is coming to an end and something new is about to happen. For instance, between a harvest game and the Bible story, a leader might say, "It's good to know that God has given us so many good things. Let's thank God for these good gifts before we listen to a story about another kind of harvest."

Things to Do in Just One Minute

- One minute room-clean-up: "You have one minute to put away your art supplies and put seven scraps in the garbage. Let's go!"
- One-minute silent reflection: "Let's take a deep breath, close our eyes, and think for one minute about how we can show Jesus' love to our neighbor."
- One-minute pair share: "Turn to your neighbor and tell her three things you'd like to do this week. You have one minute each!"
- One-minute messages: "Write a sentence of encouragement to your secret pal on this file card. Hand it to me, and I'll deliver it to the right person."
- One-minute quizzes: "How many review questions can you answer in just a minute?"

Got a minute? Use a minute . . . every minute counts.

19 Funky Funday School

Teaching Sunday school is an amazingly important, serious, life-impacting task, right? After all, you're training up the next generation of Christians. Absolutely, your job is critically necessary.

But don't get so heavy-handed that children get the idea they're serving a prison camp sentence with hard labor until they've learned their lesson.

What's the message kids get when they walk into church? Are they greeted by narrow cinder-block hallways patrolled by guards who bark out the rules? Eerie music coming from dingy "cells"? Posters of a stern Jesus in strange dress with spooky eyes that seem to say "Big brother is watching"?

What can you do to communicate that the Christian journey is a joyful journey, that Christ is an awesome travel partner in a grand adventure, that the church is on the cutting edge of a revolution that will change the world?

Here are some suggestions for turning Sunday school into Funday school:

1. Redecorate your meeting room.

- Tear down the yellowed newsprint mural and last year's visual aids, and design a fresh space that says welcome to your kids.
- Contact church agencies and request colorful posters that communicate your church's mission or feature active people working in God's kingdom.
- Design bulletin boards that feature something new each week—a joke, cartoon, community heroes, good news.
- Add living things to your space: plants, aquarium, a single flower in a bud vase.
- Create a prayer corner, a small "holy place"—perhaps partitioned from the rest of the room with a folding screen.

- Create visual interest: hang a mobile or banner, create a prayer request wall, stick a biblical timeline around the room, display artifacts from mission fields.
- Create a meeting circle by buying a blanket from a secondhand store and cutting it into a large circle; roll it up for storage.

2. Give your group a unique identity.

Dream up a cool name for the group ("The Rock Climbers," "Team 3:16"); develop a group cheer, a secret signal, a ritual greeting. You don't have to do all this yourself—invite kids to brainstorm and create their own identity. Working together on a project delivers a bonus: a feeling of community. The sky's the limit: T-shirts sporting their coat of arms, hats, pins, stationery . . .

3. Find a cause to care about and work toward a goal together.

Prisoners endure . . . but kids who learn, grow. And kids grow most if they do something about an issue, rather than just learn about it. Capitalize on children's passions; if they're upset by a news story about a baby who starved to death in a downtown rooming house, use it as a hook to get involved in a project that addresses hunger. You might, for instance, suggest a food drive in which they enlist the congregation's help to collect 100 jars of peanut butter in four weeks.

These three suggestions might inspire others. Remember, your goal is to turn an ordinary Sunday school into a Funday school. So add funky and stir. Show children that church is not a prison but an idea incubator, a learning lab, a hall of hope, a happening place where there's a buzz. That's seriously cool!

20 Talk to Me!

What do kids do best in a classroom? Talk and move. Yet what do teachers often want them to do? Be quiet and sit still. Something's wrong with this picture.

Talking is a basic developmental task for children. Babies learn to talk by cooing and babbling. Toddlers imitate words they hear and put them together into sentences; they begin asking incessant Why? questions and learn how the world functions. They play-act roles with peers and figure out more about relationships between people. Talking is an integral part of growing, learning, changing, exploring.

And that's really what Sunday school is all about. We want kids to grow spiritually, learn more about our wonderful God, change and conform to God's image, and explore what they are being called to become.

A study by educator Dr. Ned Flanders revealed that *teacher-talk in a school classroom comprises between 70-90 per cent of classroom interaction.* In a Sunday school classroom the percentages may be a little better, but too often children are discouraged from talking to you or their peers.

What's the value of kids talking? Learning is a social process—it involves checking your understanding against what others perceive. It's an active process, involving conversation, questions, rephrasing for clarification, discussion, and argument. By talking things through, children identify gaps in their own knowledge and acquire new information.

Growth and change occur when children are participating in the learning process. And that includes talking—lots of it. When the teacher is doing all the talking, the only things that may be growing are the teacher's ego and the students' apathy.

Listen to the wisdom of this Chinese proverb: "I hear, and I forget. I see, and I remember. I do, and I understand." Psychologists say we can only retain up to 10 percent of what we hear. Adding visual aids may boost our retention to 50 percent; but adding doing to the mix—and that includes talking, discussion, and role-playing—will raise that retention to 90 per cent. Says Christian educator Howard Hendricks, "Unfortunately the bulk of Christian education is hearing oriented. That's why it's often so inefficient."

Of course, you want to keep your children talking about the right things. So here are some ideas for keeping your kids talking, learning, and growing:

- Pair share: ask a question, then have the children discuss it in pairs.
- Use a talking circle/talking stick: gather children in a circle, sitting on the floor. Ask a discussion question, then pass a "talking stick" to a child. Whoever has the talking stick can talk. The talking stick goes around and across the circle as children volunteer to contribute their ideas.
- Brainstorm.
- Have kids retell the Bible story to the whole group or in small groups.
- Invite questions, and invite children to answer each other's questions.
- Initiate debates.
- Encourage kids to share stories about their week and prayer requests.
- Invite kids to teach part of a session—lead the singing, pray, read the Bible story.
- Have kids interview each other, you, or a special guest.

Your classroom may be noisier when kids talk, but noise is a small price to pay for increased involvement, learning, and the joy of discovery. "Where did we get the idea that God loves 'shhh' and 'drab' and 'anything will do'"? asks poet and Presbyterian elder Ann Weems (quoted by Marlene LeFever in *Creative Teaching Methods,* Cook Communications, 1985, 1986). "I think it's blasphemy not to bring our joy into his church."

Amen!

21 Listen Up!

God made people with two ears and only one mouth. As we've already noted, however, teachers often talk much more than listen. Yet one of the most precious gifts you can give to a child is to listen to him.

Listen to me, say your kids. Listen to my worries, my fears, my joys, my anger, my questions. Listen, really listen! When you listen to me, you tell me I am important. When you listen to me, you are modeling God's gracious listening ears. You show me that God listens when I pray. When you listen to me, really listen to me, you give me permission to ask important questions and explore my faith.

Listening involves more than ears . . . It also involves our heart, mind, and will. In a "Family Circus" cartoon, the little girl is looking at her daddy, who is reading the newspaper. She tugs at his sweater and says, "Daddy, you need to listen to me with your eyes as well as your ears."

Listening does not come naturally to most of us. But it is a skill that can be learned. Here are some important elements of active listening:

1. Listen with your whole body. Maintain eye contact. Gesture, nod, smile; lean into the conversation. Do whatever you can to show the child you are engaged with her. Kids need to know that all of you is listening, not only to their words but also to their hearts.

2. Watch for body language that reflects more than what the child is saying. Only a small part of communication is revealed through words. Drooping shoulders and folded arms speak volumes. So do sparkling eyes and dancing toes.

3. Give kids permission to talk. Begin conversations with open-ended starters: "Tell me about your day" or "I wonder how you feel about your sick dog." Often children need to be encouraged to talk, to know that you are really interested.

4. Do not interrupt. Listening takes patience. Children have a more limited vocabulary and take longer to express themselves than adults. Also, speaking about their concerns makes them vulnerable; an interruption may squash their hesitant attempts to share their ideas or thoughts.

5. Don't formulate your response while the child is still talking. Children can read eyes and body language very quickly . . . they'll know if you've tuned out.

6. Ask questions for clarification if you're not sure you're hearing the essence of what the child is saying. Rephrase what you think you're hearing, then ask, "Is this what you're saying, or am I getting it wrong?"

7. Reflect children's feelings. Often children can't name their feelings with words, or are afraid to name them. You can help by speaking for them. When you say, "It sounds like you are sad that your friend has found a new buddy to hang out with," your expression may bring relief that an unspoken feeling has been validated.

8. Ask for kids' opinions regularly. (They definitely have them!) How do they feel about war? What do they think is the most important problem world leaders should solve? When you ask for their opinions, it shows you respect their ideas. Bonus: you learn a lot about your children.

9. Share your own questions and problems (in age-appropriate ways, of course): "I'd really like to redecorate this classroom, but I don't know where to begin. Do you have any ideas?" Or, "Can anyone explain the rules of soccer to me? I'm trying to learn the game."

10. Extend conversations by asking good questions that reveal more about the child's world.

When adults model good listening, children learn essential communication skills. The greatest audience a child can have is a caring, thoughtful, interested adult who is important to them. That's you!

22 Move It!

Imagine what would have happened if Jesus had taken his followers into a classroom, seated them in rows, and lectured them about the kingdom of heaven. Suppose they all dutifully took notes and completed workbook sheets. Could they have become effective disciples by passing a test, or reciting the assigned memory work? Not likely!

Jesus knew what he was doing when he expected his motley crew of followers to get their hands dirty as they learned about the rudiments of discipleship. They chatted as they fished, acted as crowd control during healings, rustled up food and donkeys to support Jesus as he carried out his ministry. Their apprenticeship involved action as well as observation, questions, discussions, and listening.

Jesus didn't have a flannelboard, worksheets, or gold stars to assist his lesson presentations. The world was his lab, and, as Jesus' partners, the disciples pulled on their own backpacks and set out to do his bidding.

Too often Sunday school gives kids a passive learning experience: we expect them to sit and listen. Jesus used active learning principles in his "classroom." Passive learning is predictable. Active learning involves new discoveries. Passive learning is boring. Active learning is an adventure. Passive learning encourages spectators. Active learning gets everyone out on the playing field.

Active learning means indulging liberally in role-play, group work, games, simulations, field trips, service projects, drama, debates, panel discussions, action rhymes, puppetry, brainstorming, experiments, and more.

OK, you say, I surrender. I know active learning is important. But doesn't it take extra planning? Isn't active learning a risky business? If children have too much fun, will they get anything out the session? How can I be sure that I'll get all the information covered? It's noisy, and I may lose control. And when an active learning activity flops, the failures are often spectacular. How will I survive?

These are valid questions. Whenever you step out of stiff lecture shoes into action sneakers, you're taking a risk. You may need to do extra work to prepare for your class. You won't always know if kids will get what you think is important information. It could be noisy, and you may lose control. Occasionally, your carefully planned activity will flop.

But your goal is not primarily to save time, to control kids, to dole out important information in measurable doses, or to get a reputation as a grand success. The goal of your efforts is helping kids grow and learn so they will become joyful disciples of Jesus. To achieve that goal, you'll do whatever it takes.

Which would you be more likely to remember: the lecture on three ways Joseph was faithful, or sitting under a black blanket so you could imagine what it felt like to be alone in a pit? What would make a bigger impression—the worksheet on hunger statistics, or the 30-hour famine you experienced with your group? What would make a bigger impact—reading a story about a missionary in the slums, or visiting a homeless shelter downtown?

Kids—and adults too!—learn by doing. What activities can be part of your teaching so children are engaged in actively learning God's story? Try one this week!

Roll 'Em: Using Technology in the Classroom

Remember the reel-to-reel tape recorder? The filmstrip projector?

They used to be state-of-the-art teaching resources. Now they're passe. Reel-to-reel was replaced by 8-tracks, then audiocassettes. A decade ago, CDs replaced audiocassettes. Now they're being replaced by DVDs. The filmstrip projector replaced still pictures but was replaced in its turn by the film projectors, videos and DVDs.

Is technology just another word for the latest fad? Do you really need it in the classroom?

Yes . . . and no.

Nothing can replace a living, loving, caring teacher when it comes to imparting the truths of God's Word. A teacher teaches from the heart, models the truth, and is a living example of God's love. Technology cannot take over the task of teaching.

But technology is a tool that can greatly heighten the effectiveness of the words you speak. Remember, the more senses involved in learning, the better a child will remember what has been taught. Technology that encourages kids to use sight, touch, smell, and taste as well as hearing enhances your sessions; it's useful when it involves children more deeply in learning by encouraging movement and doing.

Rapid changes in this field mean that it's hard for curriculum to incorporate the most up-to-date ideas. So you'll want to do some creative thinking outside the box to incorporate the benefits of new technology. As you consider how you might use technology in your class, consider the following as well:

■ Technology is only a tool. It should never dictate the content of the lesson.
■ Technology is not necessarily a timesaver. You may need extra preparation time to learn how to use the equipment, think of a meaningful application, cue up DVDs, or follow up with editing or copying.

Here are some suggestions for bringing technology into the classroom and enhancing your lessons:

Computers and the Internet: take virtual tours of the holy land; conduct wire-side chats with missionaries; use as source of art, information, photographs; e-mail pen pals around the world; construct and maintain a class website; prepare and present PowerPoint presentations; keyboard in stories, prayers, prayer requests.

It's important to note that children routinely use e-mail to communicate with each other. So why not get into the loop? Use group e-mail to send out reminders, memory work prompts, prayer requests and assignments; send out individual e-mails to children who need encouragement or who have missed a class. It's an easy way to extend your involvement with kids outside the classroom walls.

Movies: Use brief clips as discussion or debate starters; find movies that tell Bible stories or depict practical applications of stories.

Motion pictures and videos are fully protected by copyright. However, under the fair use copyright law, teachers in a not-for-profit setting may legally use *brief* excerpts from copyrighted materials in their class sessions. If you are uncertain whether film clips you plan to use are permissible under the "fair use" guideline, either consult a lawyer in your church or apply for a blanket licensing agreement from Christian Video Licensing International (www.cvli.com) for as little as $45 per year.

Cameras: use group or individual pictures of children as prayer reminders; send pictures to shut-ins or missionaries along with letters; record activities and share with the congregation on a bulletin board; create PowerPoint presentations using photos of your class in action for congregational meetings, worship, reports to your church council, and so on.

Video cameras: record classroom dramas and share film with another group or use as story review; record greetings and songs for shut-ins and missionaries; compile a prayer-request video; record children reciting memory work or singing a song and use as a review tool.

Tape recorders: have children record their questions; send "oral letters" to others; record conducted interviews with guests, family members, or each other; present instructions at an activity center.

Music CDs or DVDs: provide background "mood" music; teach new songs.

Jesus was a creative teacher who used stones, wheat, and fig trees to bring the message of God's love down to earth. Think of how he might have used today's technology. What might he have done with a blender . . . a cell phone . . . text messaging . . . an electric popcorn popper? You can do it too!

24. Tales Around the Fire: The Art of Storytelling

God must love stories . . . he told so many of them.

Author Elie Wiesel goes even further. He writes, "God made man because he loves stories." Perhaps there's truth in that statement.

After all, God could have proclaimed the gospel message in twenty-five words or less: "I made you to live in relationship with me. You sinned and broke that relationship. I sent my Son Jesus to redeem you." Instead God gave us the Bible, a book that proclaims God's love and faithfulness through thousands of stories.

When you become a teacher of kids, you accept God's command to keep telling these stories, and telling them well. Telling them well is important. Jim Rayburn, founder of Young Life, said, "It's a sin to bore a kid with the gospel." God's stories are *not* boring. They're alive and have the power of a two-edged sword. A boring storyteller should be an oxymoron in God's kingdom.

So how do you become a good storyteller? Follow these steps:

1. Read the story from the Bible; then read it again . . . and again. You'll begin to notice details you never noticed before. You might try to read the story from different versions of the Bible to catch new insights. Read the Bible background in your leader's guide for yet another insight into the meaning of your story.

2. When the story is familiar, identify its four parts:
- Beginning: Like a handshake introducing a new friend, the beginning should be short and direct, initiating the listener to the character and setting: *There was a man who traveled from Jerusalem to Jericho. . . .*

- Action: This is the meat of the story. What is the story about? What happens? (*A traveler is assaulted on the road.*) What's the problem to be solved? (*How will he be rescued?*) How do the events in the story involve you and get you to care about the outcome? (*There's suspense as people we'd expect to help fail to do so; then along comes an outsider—what will he do?*)
- Climax: The high point of the story where the conflict is resolved. (*The Good Samaritan rescues the traveler. We feel great relief.*)
- Ending: Wraps up the loose threads of the story in a satisfying way. Should also be short and to the point. (*The Good Samaritan departs, leaving money for the traveler's needs, asking for nothing in return.*)

3. Write out the story as you'd like to tell it. Then practice telling it, either in front of a mirror, a tape recorder, a sympathetic audience, or all three. If you're using visual aids or props, practice when and where you will show them. Practice is very important for beginning storytellers. Practice gives confidence and settles the story in your mind.

4. Use feedback from the mirror or the audience to refine your story. Then practice again until telling the story feels as natural as talking.

5. Tell . . . and enjoy!

Enhance your effectiveness as a storyteller by following these tips:
- Dress simply. Avoid flashy jewelry, clothing, or scents that distract your listeners.
- Use your voice as an instrument. Vary the pitch (high to low), the volume (soft to loud), the speed (slow to fast), the intensity (flat, excited, sad, worried) of your voice.
- Keep props and visual aids simple. Children have huge imaginations—a pair of sandals and a walking stick will give them raw material to imagine a story's character and setting. Elaborate props may distract from the story itself.
- Use your hands, your eyes, your shoulders, your whole body to communicate the story's message, but again, keep it simple.
- Prepare cue cards if you're worried about losing track of the story. Write key words, phrases, or sentences on cards and arrange them in sequence. Use only when necessary.
- Let the story stand on its own feet. Don't add moralisms, meanings, and conclusions. Children will ponder and wonder about God's story, and the Holy Spirit will help them come to their own conclusions.
- In one African culture, a ritual chant signals the beginning of a story. "A story! A story!" says the storyteller, announcing his intention. "Let it come! Let it come!" urge the listeners.
- Let the story come. God will do the rest.

25 No-No's: Abuse Prevention Guidelines

Jesus took the nurture of children very seriously. He said, "When you receive the childlike on my account, it's the same as receiving me. But if you give them a hard time, bullying or taking advantage of their simple trust, you'll soon wish you hadn't. You'd be better off dropped in the middle of the lake with a millstone around your neck" (Matt. 18:5-7, *The Message*).

Harsh words! But abuse is a harsh issue. Feeling safe and secure is a basic human need. Little ones who are subjected to physical, sexual, or emotional abuse are deprived of that safety and security. Love and security from significant adults in their lives is the foundation of kids' image of God's love. Suffering abuse at the hands of caregivers and church workers strikes a blow at the emotional and faith development of a child.

Experts agree that child abuse is any kind of harm to a child's body, emotional pain, neglect, or use for sexual purposes that can cause injury or psychological damage to a child. Hitting, bullying, criticizing, exploitive touching, and ignoring a child can all be forms of abuse.

Many churches have instituted policies that safeguard the children in their care. Your church may have such policies already in place. Be sure to read them carefully and abide by them. They may include guidelines like these:

1. Screen and train workers. Church boards may require volunteers to undergo a criminal background check. They may insist that you be trained in their policies and sign an agreement to abide by them. Such a policy protects not only children but also workers. You will learn what kinds of behavior protect you from false allegations of abuse.

2. **Report.** If you become aware of possible abuse committed either by church workers or a child's caregivers, you must protect the child from further abuse by reporting what you know to civil or church authorities.

3. **Reduce the risks of one-to-one contact.** When a worker is alone with a child, the probability of an incident or an allegation of abuse increases. To avoid the risk,
- have two volunteers or staff present at every session.
- always ask permission of a parent if you do need to meet a child alone, and meet in a public place.
- have hall monitors for your program so children will be safer when going to the bathroom and so suspicious behavior will be observed.

4. **Practice safe and healthy touches.** Human beings thrive on touch and physical displays of affection. Unfortunately, rules are necessary for protecting children and leaders alike. Holding hands, side-by-side hugs ("A-frame hug"), and a hand on the shoulder are safer alternatives to frontal hugs and an arm around the waist. Never touch a child who seems to shy away from touches. Never, never kiss a child.

5. **Never let discipline become abuse.** Discipline becomes abuse when a child is blamed by an adult to justify discipline; when it results in pain, injury or humiliation; when one child is singled out, even though others are also behaving unacceptably; when it is administered excessively over a short period of time.

This information focuses on a lot of no's. Fortunately, there are many other behaviors to which you can say yes!

Say yes to respecting a child as an imagebearer of God, worthy of love and dignity.

Say yes to common sense, doing all you can to protect the reputation of the child and yourself.

And say yes to the fruits of the spirit: love, joy, peace, patience, kindness, goodness, faithfulness, gentleness and self-control (Gal. 5:22-23).

26 KNOW
Walking Hand in Hand: Affirming Diversity

A mom who adopted a baby from China tells this story. Her three-year-old was at day care when a toddler walked up to her and said, "Your eyes are different than mine."

It was a simple statement of fact. There's a huge diversity in God's family. Even little ones notice differences. This awareness of diversity in gender, race, ethnicity and abilities begins between ages two and five.

By the time children come to Sunday school, they've already absorbed attitudes and biases from their family and society. Sooner or later in your classroom you will encounter statements that are not as innocent as the toddler's remark about differences. Some child will make a remark, and that remark will hurt another child.

When teachers and parents are silent, the biased attitudes will grow stronger. On the other hand, speaking up about the problem and teaching about diversity can break down the wall of prejudice.

Here are some suggestions for helping you make your Sunday school a place where children experience the unbiased, unreserved love of Jesus and each other:

1. Model acceptable behaviors and attitudes. When you warmly welcome all children and show no favoritism when you ask questions, assign tasks, or hand out rewards, you are showing children that Jesus' love does not exclude anyone. Speak positively about other cultures and ways of living.

2. **Create an environment in your classroom that celebrates diversity.**
For instance:
- Create a mural of Jesus surrounded by a multiethnic group of people. Include children with obvious disabilities.
- Display pictures of Jesus created by artists from different races.
- Stock your room with books, toys, and music that reflect cultural diversity and disability awareness.
- Celebrate Christian holidays with customs of different cultures.
- Adapt activities so that children who have a disability can participate.
- Provide paper, crayons, and paints that enable children to create a variety of skin tones, hair colors, and costumes in their artwork.

3. **Speak up.** Take action when you hear racial slurs or put-downs that reflect stereotyped attitudes. Discuss what's being said or implied, and point out the pain this can cause others.

4. **Answer questions honestly.** Children will want to know why some people have different skin colors, or use adaptive aids, or speak with an accent. Silence or embarrassment speaks louder than words. If you don't know the answer, say so and promise to investigate.

5. **Teach about diversity.** Use activities and discussion to build positive images so children value differences. Point out stereotypes in movies and media. Give kids opportunities to role-play how they would handle instances of discrimination or prejudice. Invite them to sign petitions or write letters to address wrongs.

6. **Facilitate opportunities for children to interact with others** in different cultural situations. Visit other churches, invite visitors to you class, or attend a cultural event as a group. People often fear what they do not know, especially if they've had little exposure to people who come from different backgrounds.

At Pentecost, thousands of people of different cultures became one because of the Holy Spirit of God. Your group may be small, but you, too, can experience beautiful Pentecost unity, which is a great foretaste of what's in store for us in heaven.

—This material was first printed in *Sunday School That Really Works,* Faith Alive Christian Resources.

27 Signs of Life: Using Rituals and Symbols

The first followers of Christ knew that their lives were in danger if they openly expressed their faith, so they communicated with each other in secret. One of the symbols they used was a fish; the letters of the Greek word *ichthus,* or fish, formed an acrostic for the phrase "Jesus Christ, Son of God, Savior." They'd draw a fish in the dust, or cast it in metal and wear it on a chain, or embroider it on their clothing. And whenever they saw that fish symbol, they were affirmed and encouraged in their faith. They remembered that Jesus had called them to be fishers of men, and that he'd fed a multitude with loaves and fishes. They were members of a community of followers of Jesus.

Celebrating rituals and using signs identifies participants as members of a group and reminds them of the purpose of their community. When you use symbols and rituals in your sessions, kids will sense their connection to a very long line of believers. They will learn the language of the church and of faith, and they will know they are bound together with cords that cannot be broken.

The following ideas for creating and celebrating classroom rituals and incorporating symbols are taken from the book *Sign and Symbol, Word and Song* by Amy Florian (Ave Maria Press, Inc. 2001):

Ritual

1. Make ritual a part of every session. Beginning with a two- to five-minute ritual (such as a blessing, passing the peace, responsive reading, lighting a candle to indicate a moment of silent prayer) calms the children, creates an atmosphere of prayer and reverence, and draws your students into a faith experience. When celebrating a ritual, become a participant and invite children to take turns leading it.

2. **Present ritual postures and gestures,** and invite children to imitate you:
- Extend arms to the sides and lift hands to the heavens (the *orans* position) to indicate prayer.
- Touch the head, lips, and chest after listening to Scripture to indicate that God's Word is present in our minds, words, and heart.
- Lead processions, perhaps with banners and percussion instruments, to a prayer corner.
- Stand proud and tall when the Bible is being read, kneel when praying.
- Extend the hand in blessing to another person, or hold hands in a circle and pass a blessing around the circle.
- Practice laying on of hands (on shoulder or top of heads) when praying for a specific need of a person.

3. **Establish rituals to celebrate special occasions** like children's birthdays and at the beginning or end of a church school year. For instance, you could measure the children's height at the beginning and end of a year to indicate growth, reminding children they grow not only physically but also spiritually. Or have children take a pledge of commitment and sign a book at the beginning of a course of study.

Symbols
Include some or all of these as part of your classroom decor:
- Bible, preferably on its own table, attractively highlighted with a cloth and flowers.
- Transparent pitcher and bowl with water—a symbol of baptism and forgiveness; a small jug of oil (olive oil scented with vanilla, for instance) as a symbol of healing. Use in rituals of blessing each other or in prayers for healing.
- Candles in different colors for the liturgical seasons to light at the beginning of class or at the beginning of prayer.
- Flowers and plants, symbols of life and growth. Perhaps plant seeds or cuttings the first Sunday of a new church school season and watch the plant grow throughout the year.

28 Teaching Children to Pray

Jesus, I feel very near to you.
I feel like you are beside me all the time.
Please be with me on Thursday. I am running in a three-mile race then.
I will need all the speed in the world. If you are not busy with other things,
maybe you could be at the starting line, the finish line, and everywhere
in between.
—Frankie, age 11

—from *Dear God* by David Heller (Doubleday, 1987)

The simplicity and trust children bring to prayer reminds us that God has given them a central place in his kingdom. "See that you do not look down on one of these little ones," says Jesus to his disciples.

God loves to communicate with his children—young and old. If they talk, God will listen; if they listen, God will talk. And that's really what prayer is all about.

Here's how to encourage children to keep praying in your classroom:

1. Children learn by example. Do you pray? (Check out pp. 72-73 for ways to grow in your prayer life.)

2. Remember that childlike prayer is still real prayer—your goal is not to teach children to pray adult prayers (complete with cliches, "holy" language, and pietistic expressions). Encourage children to come to God in their own way, to do what comes naturally in a simple, conversational way. They need to know that their prayers will not be laughed at or pronounced cute or sweet.

3. Help children understand the purpose of prayer: prayer is how we build a relationship with God. Just as relationships with parents and friends grow when we talk often and openly, so we will grow closer to God by communicating regularly. And just as we talk to our families about a variety of things, so in prayer we come to God with praise, confessions, thanks and requests.

4. Learn by doing: Involve children in a multitude of prayer modes:
- Popcorn prayers: short, spontaneous, sentence prayers on a specific topic.
- Prayer journals: blank books to record children's written and drawn prayers.
- Prayer walks: a walk through the community or the church with stops along the way to pray for specific needs.
- Prayer songs: graces, blessings, the Lord's Prayer, or psalms put to music.
- Times of silence: children prepare their hearts and minds to meet God.
- Prayer request boards: mounting requests and answers to prayer in a public place.
- Prayer circles with a candle: a votive candle is passed around the circle; the child holding the candle prays aloud or silently.
- Unison prayers: memorized prayers such as the Lord's Prayer are prayed aloud together.

5. Teach children prayer methods they can do on their own at home. The ACTS acrostic is a common one (Adoration, Confession, Thanksgiving, and Supplication.) Or consider the Hand Prayer:

Thumb: strongest finger. Thank God for all the strong things in your life, like home, family, and friends.

Index: pointer finger. Pray for the people and things in your life who guide and help you: friends, teachers, doctors, nurses, pastors, and so on.

Middle: tallest finger. Pray for people who have power in this world: government, president, prime minister, mayor, and so on.

Ring: the weakest finger; it cannot do much by itself. Pray for the poor, the weak, the helpless, the hungry, the sick, and the bereaved.

Pinkie: smallest and last finger. Pray for yourself.

Note: For more prayer ideas, check out *The Praying Church Sourcebook* and *The Praying Church Idea Book,* both by Faith Alive Christian Resources.

29 Taking Stock

This quiz is a very unofficial, nonscientific checklist to help you evaluate yourself. It focuses on three areas of classroom management and shows you where you're doing well and where you might need to improve.

Check the statements that apply to you. Then read the analysis on page 65:

- ☐ I like children. ♥
- ☐ I see the world as a child sees it. ♥
- ☐ I begin preparation for teaching with prayer. 📋
- ☐ I speak to disruptive children individually and privately to determine the root of the problem. 💡
- ☐ I am aware of and use audiovisual resources available in my church. 📋
- ☐ The children in my group know what I expect of them. 💡
- ☐ I am sensitive to the needs of children and to what they are feeling and thinking. ♥
- ☐ I arrive in my classroom before the children. 📋
- ☐ I give of myself in love, time, and service. ♥
- ☐ I understand the concept of multiple intelligences and incorporate a variety of learning activities to try to reach every child's strengths. 💡
- ☐ I believe it's just as important to rejoice over good behavior as it is to discipline misbehaviors. 💡
- ☐ I am aware of the materials available in the supply cupboard. 📋
- ☐ I love Jesus, and I want to use the gifts he's given to me for God. ♥
- ☐ I understand that children's attention spans are about one minute for each year (a five-year old can focus for about five minutes on one activity.) 💡
- ☐ I make sure that there are adequate supplies to complete the activities. 📋
- ☐ I make a personal study of the lesson before preparing to teach it to the children. 📋

- ☐ I have regular times of Bible study and prayer so I can grow as a Christian. ♥
- ☐ I enforce a few basic rules consistently. 💡
- ☐ I try to learn as much personal information about each child as possible. 📋
- ☐ I treat children with as much love and respect as I do adults. ♥
- ☐ I will never, never, never hit a child. 💡
- ☐ I believe that there are reasons for each misbehavior and try to discover them. 💡
- ☐ My heart's desire is to become all that Christ wants me to be. ♥
- ☐ I know who I can ask to substitute teach for me in an emergency situation. 📋
- ☐ I evaluate the curriculum and adapt sessions to meet my group's needs. 📋
- ☐ I pray for the children in my group. ♥
- ☐ I lower my voice rather than raising it when addressing a noisy group. 💡
- ☐ I consult with other teachers and leaders if I have questions. 📋
- ☐ I understand that I need to have a loving relationship with each child in my care. ♥
- ☐ I use language that is age-appropriate and explain unfamiliar words. 💡

Check boxes of the statements that describe you *most or all of the time*. Be honest, but also kind to yourself. Nobody is perfect, and you can't measure up perfectly. If you're attempting to fulfil the statements, give yourself the benefit of the doubt.

Tally up the scores for each category:

___ ♥

___ 📋

___ 💡

Hearts: These measure your heart commitment to God and to your children. If you have less than six heart boxes checked, ask yourself if you really want to be teaching children. Children store up impressions and feelings in Sunday school that become an important part of the groundwork for their faith walk. As a teacher, you teach the child in everything you do, including your attitudes, your casual words and looks, and your attitudes. You become a model to these children. That's important business, not to be taken lightly.

Clipboards: These measure the important task of lesson preparation. If you have less than six boxes checked in this area, you should recognize that teaching requires time and effort outside of the classroom as well as in it. Good preparation shows that you value church education and are prepared to take the time it needs to do it well. Take the time . . . and reap the rewards.

Lightbulbs: These measure how familiar you are with disciplinary techniques in the classroom. If you have less than six boxes checked in this category, take heart! Classroom management is a skill that can be learned. These ten questions only scratch the surface. There are many courses you can take and books you can read to help you. Observing experienced teachers also helps.

If your heart is in the right place, and you are taking the time that's necessary to prepare, and you're willing to learn, you're well on your way to being a teacher who lives on in the fond memories of the children.

Real Teachers Do Eat Crow: Dealing with Failures

Failure happens to everyone. Everyone. No exceptions.

Class attendance drops. The kids seem bored. Or they run all over you. The lesson you worked on so hard fell flat. Children challenge you with questions you can't answer. The unhappy child you've been praying for has dropped out of class. A feisty kid says flat-out that he doesn't believe in God anymore, and the rest of the kids seem to admire him. Teaching Sunday school feels like a thorn in the flesh. Are you really making a difference?

In his book *Help! I'm a Sunday School Teacher!* (Youth Specialties, 1995) Ray Johnston gives some good advice:

> *Failure is never fatal—but discouragement can be! When I bomb (and it happens regularly), I find that two reminders keep me going.*
>
> *First, no teacher can connect with every kid. No Sunday school teacher is interesting every week. And no Sunday school teacher is liked by all the kids. You will have kids that are too cool, too flaky, or too bored—or they just won't like you. Give yourself a break. Chances are, if you are really honest, you don't like every kid either.*
>
> *Second, no kid is beyond God's reach. Have you thought about the disciples lately? Doubting Thomas, loud-mouthed Peter, and James and John always arguing over who was the greatest. Sound familiar? The next time you are ready to throw in the towel, remember the disciples and trust God to use you to reach your students in his timing.*

It's not about you . . . it's about God. And God does know what he is doing. Failure is an opportunity to live out a lesson you want your kids to learn: trust and obey.

And while you're doing that, hang on to this promise:

As the rain and the snow come down from heaven,
and do not return to it without watering the earth
and making it bud and flourish,
so that it yields seed for the sower and bread for the eater,
so is my word that goes out from my mouth:
It will not return to me empty,
but will accomplish what I desire
and achieve the purpose for which I sent it.
You will go out in joy and be led forth in peace;
the mountains and hills will burst into song before you,
and all the trees of the field will clap their hands.
Instead of the thornbush will grow the pine tree,
and instead of briers the myrtle will grow.
This will be for the LORD's renown,
for an everlasting sign which will not be destroyed.
—Isaiah 55:10-13

Scout's Honor: The Need for Transparency and Honesty

Transparency isn't just another name for an overhead—it's also an essential quality of a good teacher.

Transparent teachers have nothing to hide—they're open and honest. Transparent teachers are not spending their energy wearing a mask that hides their real selves.

Genesis 3, the story of how Satan tempted Adam and Eve to sin, teaches that the essence of evil is deceitfulness and lies. Teachers of children cannot live a lie or mislead the children they've promised to lead. To do so may be to cause Jesus' kids, the ones he loved and died for, to stumble. Paradoxically, if you're not transparent, kids can see through you.

Here's how you can cultivate honesty in your life:

1. Be honest with God. God wants and asks for all of your heart commitment. Christians are people on the way—they are not perfect. You're not asked to be a perfect role model—just a living, growing child of God. God's people are committed to letting God be the king of their lives; they desire always to root out the sin that creeps into their hearts. If you examine your heart and realize there are still parts of it that are not submitted to God, confess your sin and ask for the Spirit's help.

2. Be honest with yourself. God knows that you will sometimes be tired, discouraged, ready to throw in the towel. You will not always be "up" and full of excitement about the work you are doing. Sometimes you won't even like those kids much (gasp!). You'll wonder if this job is right for you. So don't pretend to be the perfect saint, always eager to do good works. When you admit those negative feelings to yourself, you've taken the first step in dealing with them. You'll be able to share your feelings with God and with God's people. That's where help comes from. Being honest with yourself is the beginning of growth and change.

3. **Be honest with your leaders.** Church leaders who organize children's programs are always looking for volunteers. That's you! It's up to you to let them know when you have questions, problems, doubts, or frustrations. It's not in anyone's best interest to hide these issues. If you feel like you need more training, if the supplies you were promised don't materialize, if you feel like you're serving a life sentence because you haven't been given time off, speak up. Be honest. Don't hide problems where they'll fester and cause anger or discouragement.

4. **Be honest with children.** No, you don't have to bare your souls and confess your darkest sins to them. But you should be able to say honestly that you are a sinner, that you do have questions, that sometimes you struggle. If they raise an issue and you don't know the answer, say so. If they catch you in an inconsistency, admit it. If something is troubling you—your mother's cancer, your spouse's unemployment, or your runaway dog—say so. The bonus is that when you become vulnerable, kids are more likely to come to you with their own problems.

And they just might surprise you—by sending a card to your mother, praying for your spouse, or making a poster to advertise your lost dog.

32 Rest Stops: Remember to Take a Breather

Hiking is hard work. That's why you'll find rest stops along the trail. Teaching children is hard work too. You'll need to balance your hard work with adequate time for rest. Jesus says, "Catch your breath! Take a break. Come apart and be with me a while" (see Mark 6:31).

In his book *Rest,* Dr. Siang-Yang Tan describes four areas of our lives that need rest: physical, emotional, relational, and spiritual. Busy people need to take care of their bodies, giving them enough—but not too much—food, sleep, exercise, and leisure. They need to give their minds a rest so they can experience emotional peace, quiet, contentment, and serenity. Busy people need to find relational harmony with others, including fellowship and deep friendships that are experienced in community. Most of all, busy people need to find rest from guilt, doubt, and emptiness by living in faith.

It's a matter of obedience. God gave a command—not a suggestion—that his people observe Sabbath rest. Sabbath is not a synonym for the pursuit of leisure or amusement, but rather a genuine time of refreshment for body, mind, and spirit. It is time when God's children rest from their work, wait in stillness before him, and drop stresses at his feet.

It's a matter of necessity. Scripture teaches clearly that there is a God-created rhythm to periods of work followed by times of rest. The same rhythm exists in creation: night leads to day, seasons follow upon each other, tides flow in and out, body organs have a pattern of working and resting. God instituted the Sabbath, the year of Jubilee, celebrations, and festivals because he knew we need times of rest in order to survive and grow. Plants go into periods of dormancy, only to burst into new life after a period of rest. Rest is a necessity for those who give of themselves to others.

It's a matter of joy! Doing nothing gets a bad rap these days—action and accomplishment appear much superior to inactivity or waiting. The anthem of today's society appears to be "Hurry, hurry, hurry; rush, rush, rush; more, more, more." And the result—evident in increasing numbers of stress-related illnesses and psychological problems—is loss of joy. God has an antidote: Rest and recapture joy. "You have made known to me the path of life; you will fill me with joy in your presence, with eternal pleasures at your right hand" (Ps. 116:11).

How do we rest when there is so much work to do? Take a lesson from Jesus: he did not ask permission when he withdrew to a quiet place to pray. He was obeying his heavenly Father's command and call. There were still people begging to be healed, lessons to be taught, disciples to lead, yet Jesus would spend time, instead, praying or having dinner with friends.

Perhaps you have been teaching Sunday school for years and years and years without a break. Perhaps you are neglecting your own family to take care of the church's children. Perhaps your body, your emotions, your relationships, and your soul are suffering from want of rest. To you, God says, "Take a break. I'm telling you, just do it. You need to rest. It will be good for you. Trust me."

33. Power Walking: Cultivating a Prayer Life

How important is prayer? Listen . . .

Pray without ceasing.
—the apostle Paul

Prayer is the mortar that holds our house together.
—Mother Teresa

Prayer is the sum of our relationship with God. We are what we pray.
—Carlo Carretto

Prayer does not change God, but it changes him who prays.
—Soren Kierkegaard

I believe that true prayer makes us into what we imagine. To pray to God leads to becoming like God.
—Henri J. M. Nouwen

Seven days without prayer makes one weak.
—Anonymous

How important is prayer? Christians from all times and places testify it is absolutely essential. "You can do more than praying after you have prayed," says Corrie Ten Boom. "You can never do more than praying before you have prayed."

Prayer is about growth and change. To pray is to be open to the Spirit of God working in you. And growth is what you desire for yourself and for the children you teach as you model Christ's love.

How do busy people with lots of work to do find the time to pray? The secret is to pray as you *are*, not as you *ought*. There's no one "right" way to approach God—there are many. God made us all different, and we are all in different life situations. The retired senior may find that a long morning "quiet" time is the best way to pray, while a busy mom of three preschoolers can only pray as she wipes sticky hands and rocks babies to sleep. A businessman may turn a rail car into a prayer chapel as he uses his fifty-minute commute to pray. A writer turns to the computer, a laborer kneels at the bedside last thing at night, and an administrator keeps a small altar of stones on a filing cabinet as a reminder to pray for every client that comes through the office.

If you are having difficulty sustaining a prayer life to nourish your soul and to keep you connected to God, be encouraged by these bits of advice from well-known Christian thinkers:

> *Prayer is an unnatural activity. . . . Prayer is alien to our proud human nature. And yet somewhere, someplace, probably all of us reach the point of falling on our knees . . . we pray because by intuition or experience, we understand that the most intimate communion with God comes only through prayer.*
> —Bill Hybels, *Too Busy Not to Pray* (InterVarsity Press, 1998), pp. 9-10

> *We should remember that God always meets us where we are and slowly moves us along into deeper things. Occasional joggers do not suddenly enter an Olympic marathon. They prepare and train themselves over a period of time, and so should we. When such a progression is followed we can expect to pray a year from now with greater authority and spiritual success than at present.*
> —Richard Foster, *Celebration of Discipline* (Harper San Francisco, 1988), p. 35

> *[God] wants more than an appointment in your schedule. He wants to be included in every activity, every conversation, every problem, and even every thought. You can carry on a continuous open-ended conversation with him throughout your day, talking with him about whatever you are doing or thinking at that moment.*
> —Rick Warren, *The Purpose Driven Life* (Zondervan, 2002), p. 87

> *When I talk to Jesus, he bends down to hear me.*
> —Larry, age 9, quoted in *Jesus Is . . .* by Lenore Johnson (Harper and Row, 1971)

As you prepare each session, you may want to begin by praying this prayer, based on Colossians 1:-14, Paul's prayer for the people he was teaching:

Lord, I thank you for _____. *[name the children you teach]*
I thank you for the faith, hope, and love that are springing up in their hearts.
I thank you that your gospel is bearing fruit and growing.
I thank you for the people who have taught me so that I can teach others.
Lord, I pray for each child in my group: for _____ *[name the children you teach again]* and for myself as I teach this session.
I pray that you will fill us with the knowledge of your will.
I pray for spiritual wisdom and understanding.
I pray that we may live a life worthy of you,
that we will please you by bearing fruit
growing in knowledge,
being strengthened with power.
I pray that we will have endurance and patience,
that we will joyfully give thanks for all things.
Thank you for rescuing us from darkness and bringing us into your Son's kingdom,
in whom we have redemption and forgiveness of sins. Amen.

34   Stretching Keeps You Limber

Would you sign up for a fitness class with an instructor who barks out exercise moves while slouching in a recliner and chowing down on candy bars and chips? Not likely.

Would you take your car to a mechanic who has a wrench in one hand and *Quicky Car Repair for Amateurs* in the other? Hire a salesman who doesn't know a shingle from a showroom to repair your roof? Pay good money to take a university chemistry class from a professor whose thesis was on Victorian poets? No, no, and no again.

People expect that those who provide a service have expertise to meet specific needs. That applies to Sunday school teachers too: your kids will expect you to speak from experience when you teach. They'll expect you to walk your talk. Christian teachers, especially, must speak from their hearts so as not to bring dishonor to God's name.

Do you want your children to grow and learn? Then be sure that you are a model of growing and learning.

"The effective teacher always teaches from the overflow of a full life," writes Christian educator Howard Hendricks in *Teaching to Change Lives*. "The Law of the Teacher, simply stated, is this: If you stop growing today, you stop teaching tomorrow."

You are on a journey, and you have not arrived! As long as you are still breathing, there are things left to learn. This has nothing to do with age and everything to do with attitude. The hunger you have for learning is contagious—your kids will catch it from you. It's a great condition to have!

Consider these ways to keep growing:

1. **Grow in Bible knowledge and understanding.** This is the root of your belief and behavior. Nourish your soul with God's Word every day.

2. **Grow in community.** Your community of faith is a great source of challenge, encouragement, and understanding. God's church is a body, and its members are meant to supply each other's needs. Be part of a class, a small group, a prayer cell, or a task force to keep you stretched.

3. **Grow in skills.** The world of education is a big world. Even the most experienced teachers can benefit from training. Take advantage of conferences, seminars, and workshops to learn new techniques, insights, and discoveries that will enhance your teaching.

4. **Grow in knowledge.** Read books and magazines or surf the web to learn more about children's development, new curriculum, and the latest information about the world we live in. All of this information will make you a better teacher.

5. **Grow in grace.** The best teacher realizes how much he or she still has to learn. Grace for the journey means that you are teachable.

Remember, a well-conditioned teacher suffers less pain on the trail and experiences more joy. For God's sake, and for your own, exercise your mind, stretch yourself, and stay limber.

35 Pack Out What You Pack In

True or false: If we can persuade children to believe the right things, they will act in the right way.

Wrong! Sounds good on paper, but living the faith isn't quite as simple as just believing the right things. The sad fact is, people who believe gluttony is a sin still overeat, and people who know murder is wrong still kill others with their words.

It's important to teach what the Bible says. But it's even more important to give children opportunities to put their beliefs into practice. Children who learn to live their faith develop holy habits that stay with them long after the teacher has left the classroom.

Here are some important things to think about as you help kids walk the talk of faith:

1. Don't give children all the answers. You might be tempted to sum up your lessons with a stated conclusion or moral, but that doesn't necessarily teach children enough. Instead, ask good questions that help them think for themselves. Guide them to consider how they can apply their learning to their lives. Challenge them to think for themselves, to internalize their learning. Instead of saying, "We've learned from Ananias and Sapphira that Jesus is unhappy when we lie. So from now on, let's please Jesus by telling the truth!" ask, "When are you tempted to lie? What could you do the next time you are tempted to lie?"

2. Role-play. Let kids practice a lesson application by acting it out with each other. Although the situation may be artificial, it allows them to try it on for size, and to refine future actions. Instead of "Today, when you go home, do something to show your family you love them," say, "Before we go home, we are going to practice what we will do to show love to our family. First you will choose a partner. Tell each other which action you will do. Then show your partner how you will do this."

3. **Encourage children to make specific commitments.** Commitments invite children to affirm their beliefs by agreeing to act in concrete ways. Be sure to follow up to ensure that children are fulfilling their commitments. Instead of saying, "Each of us should think about something we can do and report back next week about the results," say, "For the next five minutes, write about or draw a picture of one thing you will do differently this week. Put your commitment in an envelope with your name on it. Before you go home, we'll pray about these commitments. Next week, we will open the envelopes and see how well you have done."

4. **Engage children in group service projects.** "Service projects are not only the best cure for "me-itis," but they are also the natural response to many lessons we already teach in children's ministry; they allow us to take our students beyond simply hearing, talking about, or even planning ways to love and obey God. Service projects motivate students to action: loving and obeying God as they assist others" (*The Big Book of Service Projects,* Gospel Light Publishing, 2001). Instead of saying, "God wants us to show love for those who are needy," say, "Three seniors in our church neighborhood cannot do their own yard work. Next Saturday, we'll get together and do a spring clean-up for them."

Finally, here's one more absolutely essential way to encourage your children to put their faith into practice: **Be a model yourself.**

"Don't fool yourself into thinking that you are a listener when you are anything but, letting the Word go in one ear and out the other. *Act* on what you hear!" (James 1:22, *The Message*).

Learning the Ropes: Helping Kids Develop Their Spiritual Gifts

You've probably heard people say that children are the church of tomorrow—as in, "We need to train up our children. They are the church of tomorrow!" or "Let's use musical styles that appeal to our children to keep them in church, for they will be the church of the future."

Actually, children are *not* the church of tomorrow. They are the church of today, just as much as adults are! There's no magic moment when a person is old enough to "be the church." In fact, Jesus valued children and took time to receive and bless them.

If children are the church, Christ's body, the Bible teaches that each has spiritual gifts to contribute to the body. (Read 1 Corinthians 12 again as a refresher course in how important each person in the church is to the whole.)

Children have wonderful gifts that help build up the body of believers. A four-year old kisses the cast covering the broken leg of a senior member: she's using her gifts of mercy, healing, and encouragement. A seven-year-old answers a pastor's question during the children's message in such a way that the adults in the pew are amazed—he's exercising his gift of wisdom and discernment. A ten-year-old's questions and opinions about a denominational debate cause people to rethink the controversial issue; she's got the gift of teaching. As you work with children, you too will likely benefit from their insights, ideas, actions, and questions.

How do you help children develop and use their gifts for the benefit of the church?

1. Be an encourager. Many people learn about their spiritual giftedness through the observations and affirmations of others. "You're an excellent helper, Pete!" and "You ask the most interesting questions, Joel—you make me think hard" are encouraging comments that alert children to the strengths God's Spirit has given them.

2. **Be a facilitator.** In your work with kids, you will notice strengths and gifts that may not be obvious to others in the church. If a child in your group has drawn a particularly moving picture of the crucifixion or written a beautiful poem, find ways of sharing these gifts with the rest of the congregation. Perhaps the work can be published in a church bulletin or newsletter. You may notice opportunities for your children to serve and to use their gifts in church projects, work bees, and worship services. You can make it happen by linking the need with the gifts.

3. **Be a teacher.** Introduce the language and concepts of spiritual gifts into your storytelling and teaching as opportunities arise. This can be done very simply with young children by naming different gifts and observing how Bible characters used their gifts for the Lord and for God's people. In middle school, you may wish to explore spiritual gifts. Share stories of Bible heroes and Christian saints of all sorts who used their gifts to build the church.

4. **Be a model.** You have been given gifts to use in God's kingdom. Are you serving joyfully? Are you nurturing your gifts and learning to use them more effectively by participating in ongoing training? Are you relying on God's Spirit to see you through rough times? Are you seeking support, prayers, and encouragement from the family of God to strengthen your commitment?

Whoever welcomes a little child—his smile, her energy, his creative talent, her mercy and love, his wisdom, her leadership, his helpfulness, her knowledge—like this in my name, welcomes me, says Jesus. Help your children "be the church" right now, just as they are.

37 Unplug the Teaching Machine

Here's some good news: you are not alone. There's a whole group of potential teachers in your classroom ready to share the teaching load. Who are these teachers? The children themselves.

It may not make mathematical sense, but it's perfectly true: 2 teach is 2 learn 2 times.

When your children have an opportunity to practice their learning by teaching others, they learn more.

In *Help! I'm a Sunday School Teacher!* (Youth Specialties, 1995) Ray Johnston lists other benefits to giving your children opportunities to do some of the teaching:

1. It combats apathy. Children who are actively involved don't have a chance to be bored or disruptive.

2. Children often listen better to other children than to adults (especially as they get older).

3. The act of teaching may help children discover a potential gift of leadership, teaching, or knowledge.

Begin small: have kids take turns leading in prayer, choosing songs, reading Scripture, taking attendance, and other jobs that you would normally do yourself. Be sure children understand that you are counting on them, and give them specific instructions ahead of time: "Maria, I'd like you to lead the opening litany next week. Here are the words—please take them home and practice them this week."

Review situations are good places for children to try their hand at teaching. Invite children to retell the stories in their own words, perhaps creating their own visual aids. They can write good questions and conduct a review quiz for the class. They can be referees in a game of Bible Baseball. They can also be in charge of and operate audiovisual equipment when showing a review DVD or listening to a song.

Remember that not all teaching consists of words and stories. Skills such as art, music, drama, and social interaction are often learned through observation and imitation. Consider pairing children on a regular basis: a weak reader with a stronger one, a social star with a shy child, a "wild child" with a self-disciplined one, a good artist with a less creative child. As they work on projects or assignments together, children serve as role models and helpers for each other.

Challenge kids to take charge of a specific part of your program. For instance, for a service project that involves bringing items for a food bank, children can assume responsibility for specific parts of the project: publicity (make posters and write notices for the church bulletin), donations (create a goal chart), delivery (ask parents to help deliver the items to the food bank).

Take a risk—share the teaching load with your children. If the experiment fails, you can be comforted by one thing: kids will develop a new appreciation for your job and all it involves!

38 Trail Blazing: A Look at the Future

Robert Raikes (1735-1811) is widely considered to be "Mr. Sunday School." Raikes saw how little opportunity children of working-class parents had to get an education (many of them were joining their parents in the work world six days a week). In 1780, he set up a Sunday school in his hometown of Gloucester, England, where these children could learn to read and write. He used the Bible as his textbook.

By 1831, the movement had grown across England, ministering to 1.25 million children, one quarter of the child population. The Sunday school movement changed children's lives, teaching them spiritual truths while increasing their skills in reading and writing.

Sunday school has always been about helping people grow and change. It has been used as an outreach arm of the church, preaching the gospel to unchurched children; as a supportive institution, helping parents teach their children Scriptural truths; as the only child-oriented ministry in an adult-dominated menu of services. It's been a safe haven for battle-weary children, a place where Christian beliefs have been woven into the fabric of our lives. Songs and verses learned in Sunday school have comforted soldiers in battle and inspired hospital patients on their sickbeds.

But what will the Sunday school of the future look like? Nobody really knows. But it's interesting to consider the realities of the world we live in now. These are the realities the church must consider as it plans ministries. An article by Margaret F. Williamson ("Today's Sunday School: Dead or Alive?" www.baptistcenter.com/Journal) points at some characteristics of today's world:

■ A consumer-driven culture creates trends such as *cocooning* (the stay-at-home trend), *clanning* (the desire to be together with like-minded people), and *anchoring* (reaching back to spiritual roots).

- Busyness and multiple roles are facts of life. Time is even more important than money. Sunday school has to fit into a schedule beset by time constraints.
- Society reinvents itself every three to five years. Change is inevitable, not an option.
- The population make-up of North America is changing; diversity rather than homogeneity is the norm.
- Family structures are changing: the nuclear family (working dad, stay-at-home mom, and a few children) comprises less than 10 percent of the population. The number of single-parent families and non-family households is growing quickly.
- People no longer consider the church to be the only authority in their search for spiritual truth. Alternate sources of authority include the Internet, books, television, non-Christian traditions, and personal experiences.

Such realities have implications for ministry to children. You may find that the kids in your group come from a greater variety of ethnic groups; that you cannot assume anything about their family situations; that they don't attend Sunday school regularly because it interferes with visitation rights, soccer games, or because their mom needs to sleep in. Perhaps children's parents or caregivers are checking out the church for the first time today; a sense of family or spiritual rootedness will encourage them to come back. You can't assume that these parents will spend hours every week supporting your ministry, overseeing memory work, or following up on Scripture stories or service projects.

Today's kids are nonlinear thinkers. They pick up their information in bits and pieces and fit that information into empty slots that are not necessarily connected by logic. Their view of life has been influenced by fast movies, fast videos, fast changes in society. They're very comfortable with contradictions and not especially concerned about absolute truths. We can reach these children by facilitating relationships and experiences with people they know and trust. We can reach them with technology (91 percent of teenagers use the Internet, often to build new relationships). We can reach them through music, the language of their culture. They're not impressed by lectures.

What might a Sunday school class designed to meet the needs of these children look like? Such a class would be fun—it would offer a wide mixture of activities, using technology and music as important tools. The teacher would be warm and caring, authentic and vulnerable. The program would encourage intergenerational involvement to expose kids to many different role models. It would reach outside the classroom to connect kids and teacher by cell phone, e-mail, and text messaging. The class would offer a secure atmosphere in which kids know they are free to ask questions and to explore answers. Teachers would employ a wide variety of teaching modes to reach as many children as possible.

Although children's learning styles and cultural realities may change over time, their basic human needs do not. They need someone to care, and they need someone to tell them the truth in a way that speaks to them. Jesus did it, and you can do it too.

Critics have scorned church school as being past its "best-before" date. Society has changed, they've pointed out; it's time to replace Sunday school with something else. Yet it survives . . . somewhat battered and bruised, but still vital. Children who attend it still hear the most beautiful story in the world, and they become part of that story and pass it on.